CONSCIOUSNESS

FOR

HEARTBREAK

OBSESSION

AND

PROCESS ADDICTION

BY

MICHAEL PARADIS

CONTENTS

Curative Consciousness

For

Heartbreak, Obsession, and Process Addiction

By

Michael Paradis

Preface

This book was written for the person who suffers unwanted memories and/or irrational fears that place them in a perpetual state of misery or anxiety. This unhappy state is at the core of human pathology in that it motivates destructive behavior and sense-seeking as a means of distraction or temporary escape. Life seems a storm at times, but need that tempest also reside inside us? What is the cause of enduring unhappiness? Is it merely genetics and the combination of events that come together to make us this way? Is there something beyond life-circumstances that can bring us peace? So much unhappiness is pointless, brought on by giving weight to things that are unworthy of it. The scope of such things must be drastically narrowed. It is through conditioning that we fall into this misappropriation of attention, and so the undoing of this conditioning can help us establish a more realistic reaction to life. There is a hidden blessing in desperate unhappiness in that it can motivate the inner-search for liberation.

When I started writing this book, it was because I was experiencing significant relief from having an addictive, needy personality and an extremely loud mind. The escape from these tendencies was motivated by repeated frustration in pursuing experiences and material things as a means of forgetting life's problems. My mind would constantly ruminate on both the things it wanted and the things it didn't want. My inner-narrative revolved around fears and desires. Consider the nature of your thoughts, and if you see yourself in these descriptions, I want you to keep reading, particularly if you feel like you have an obsession or unresolved issue that you cannot escape. There is a way to get out of this maze, but it might change you so profoundly that you end up feeling like a different person, and the journey is perilous, for if you successfully subordinate mental content to consciousness, it will put you out of step with the majority of people, who simply do not operate wholly in reality, but rather, in reaction to how their conditioning fits with it. You will become the original, free being, whose known self is pure love. Your eyes will be opened to a reality that is hidden to most.

Note that I am not a doctor, counselor, or therapist of any kind. This is not medical advice. I'm just someone who, through suffering, recognized a pattern of wanting that brought a boom and bust cycle of happiness through acquisition and misery through jadedness. This pattern is as conditional as the content from which it arises. You can break identification with it and be free.

A note on non-duality - There is a great deal of confusion surrounding the choice of words used to describe the ineffable; therefore, some clarifications will be helpful. Some will perceive that the author has taken license with the words "consciousness," and "mind," seemingly approaching them from a dualistic perspective. The word consciousness denotes not the state of being awake, but rather, the medium through which all forms, both subtle and gross, appear as things but are in-fact, movements. Consciousness is the medium, and what's referred to as "the Self," is consciousness in its absolute repose, the space in which all things appear and the

3

unmanifest from which all things arise. The true Self is without qualities or divisions, but its reflection in the stillness of the spiritual heart reveals that it is love. This fact is discovered in what can be described as a feeling of peace that is permanently knowable in full surrender to what is, which is the letting go of circumstances as a means to it. This is not written as speculation on the part of the author, but from the ongoing abidance in that peace, apart from which, all else are temporary states. What's taken to be a personal self is merely an illusion, a movement within the space from which it arises. It may appear that consciousness is being described as something separate from something else, but it actually denotes the stillness of consciousness that expands within the troubled consciousness that is known as a mind, which is, as all things, encompassed within the field of   consciousness.

Introduction

There are greater calamities in life, but anyone who has had a full-blown obsession knows how torturous it can be. You find yourself thinking of the same person or event, over and over, possibly for years. You find too many things that remind you of the object of your obsession, e.g., a certain song, place, or season, etc. It can ruin your life when you see no end to it. It can reach a point where the only way to not think of the obsession is to find a way to think of nothing at all.

I have struggled with process addiction, jumping from one obsession to the next, getting immersed to the point of letting it interfere with my life. I would pat myself on the back for having bested one addiction, as I dove headlong into another. I've been addicted to or obsessed with a variety of subjects and activities.

I've also been painfully obsessed with a few failed relationships. It took twenty years and two failed marriages to comprehend that there was a larger problem afoot in generating these addictions and obsessions. I was not seeing it, like a highly-compensated but broke person who doesn't understand that getting more money doesn't address their inability to spend less than they earn. I was blind to the fact that I was mismanaging my inner space, and that it was causing me to seek out addictions.

Life seemed a constant game of immersing my attention in various outside things, each one being the focus until it lost its novelty or encroached upon a relationship. This cycle created ripples of chaos and unhappiness in my life and the lives of those near me. In my religious life, I had belief but no spiritual practice beyond trying to communicate with God through prayer. I grew up thinking that if I believed the right things, took them on faith, and made an earnest effort to be a good person, I would go to heaven through God's grace. However, there was a disconnect between what I believed and the compulsions that ran me, bringing about a perpetual cycle of guilt. Guilt is a negative emotion that will separate you from joy. The negative emotions that follow unconscious actions motivate the next volley of regretful choices. Unhappiness motivates actions that bring short-lived satisfaction, followed by consequences that bring more unhappiness, and so it goes. The cycle stems from ignorance, wrongly believing ourselves to be the changeful and not the changeless space through which it moves. These movements are perceived to be separate and vulnerable things, i.e., the body and mind, and there is fear at the prospect of their passing. This fear is a distortion in consciousness that hides the very peace that's sought in pursuits that grant the illusion of security. Fear is only temporarily dampened in either the distractions of pleasure or the maintaining of ideal life-circumstances. The two aforementioned states are conditions within the changeful and are therefore, passing. Their end brings the return of fear, but their pursuit also disturbs the space, which must be unconditionally stilled to apprehend the peace that It is. In stillness, the space discovers its unchanging nature and thus, fear dissolves as the product of illusion. Only surrender to the perfection of creation's unfolding will relax the distortions that hide this truth, bringing unconditional alignment between the gross and subtle aspects of itself. In this alignment there is clarity that nurtures the expansion of stillness and the apprehension of true and unconditional peace.

If you gave everybody the same life circumstances, would they all be equally happy? Of course not! The feeling of happiness stems from an inner arrangement, not the dependence on an outer one. Life circumstances are in flux for everyone. There are ups and downs, but some people do better at handling these swings. There are happy people who have none of the trappings of life that others less-happy deem necessary. The happy do not fear losing what's known to be temporary; they enjoy it for what it is, *while* it is. But the unhappy ones view the key to happiness as conditional, derived from the outside, through ideal life circumstances. They waste their energy trying to secure the outside, while creating disturbance on the inside. Given the transitory nature of worldly things, is it realistic to expect them to sit still for our happiness? In-fact, it is the chasing of this happiness that obscures it. Why can't we be still and see this? Lasting happiness is a reflection that shines from the stillness of the spiritual heart. But the resistances of the mind distort this countenance, depicting a fearful and false reflection of form and conditioning.

The satisfaction derived from outside things is but a reflection of the joy that radiates from us when our attention is pulled from the sheath of conditioning that muffled it. It's like we're the sun that sees only the light of the moon, not knowing that its light is a reflection of our own. In our delusion, we lament its waning as that of our own joy. So really, the joy is our true nature, uncolored by any impurity. The good news is that the inner search can liberate this joy from the conditioned, illusory self. The bad news is that looking inward seems a fruitless task on the surface, as the treasures of the truth are not apparent through the layers of conditioning. When the joy is obscured by thought, we look outward for light; then when the object of distraction dissipates the clouds of thought, we see joy's reflection in the thing that grabbed our attention, hence we never recognize the unconditioned source within. We can't know what the reward of the inner-discovery will be, and so we don't put forth the effort. However, when we recognize the futility of the pleasure/pain cycle, it motivates the search in-earnest. At first, this search will still be external, looking for knowledge that holds the key to liberation. But then the seeker may find the pointing that instructs them to look inward and discover the truth.

The mental database from which you operate is not you, and it was not consciously put there by you; it came from experiences born of assigned circumstances, e.g., education, zip code, parents, friends, and "the media." The information that fills the mind forms a construct as which we identify. As we mature, this construct grows with our learning. Because we identify strongly and unconsciously with this content, we don't see it as foreign, but it's not you, for how can what's observed be the essence of *that which* observes it? You started out as a happy child who was born lacking the foreign currency of words in which the false identity is denominated. A child doesn't need much to be happy, but the more information that's added, the more that happiness will become conditional, dependent upon how that conditioning fits with reality. A reality that countervails the conditioning is feared by the one who identifies with it. It is simply hoarded information that divorces the child from their true nature.

Thoughts, emotions, and the consciousness through which they resonate, are elements of the inner-being that can be managed to produce life-changing benefits. Thoughts and emotions are just vibrations within consciousness, determining your perceived state of being to the degree that you identify with them. There is the physical, objective world of brain and body chemistry, and then there is the inner, subjective world of thoughts and emotions. They exert influence on each other, and so the problem between them can be attacked from either side, but to distill consciousness unconditionally, it must be done internally, without the use of outside props. This internal "work," which leads to effortless-inner-quietude, is the re-cultivation of an awareness that goes beyond the five senses.

There is a facet of perception that is normally clouded by thought; it is the awareness that follows your attention. In the distillation of awareness from thought-vibrations, there is the realization of unconditional peace. Normally, awareness is taking on the vibrations of thoughts to which attention is given, and hence, the peace of its natural stillness is obscured. A much greater part of this peace was apprehended in childhood and is revisited in dreams.

However, in taking on an identity, which is wholly imaginary, as well as constructing and placing attention in the timeline, also imaginary, the peace of childhood is hidden. We grow up and forget the peace that constitutes our true nature. The adult mode of finding peace is through acquisitions and experiences that temporarily liberate attention from the imaginary, allowing the peace of pure awareness to re-appear. It then disappears when the novelty of the experience diminishes, and our attention recedes from the moment and back into the vibration of our thought content, our imaginary identity. We don't see the peace as being ourselves and instead think it conditional, coming from the outside attraction. This peace is also apprehended in dreaming, as the patina of thought and emotion (the mind) becomes a world that the dreamer observes from pure awareness. Instead of carrying thought and emotion as a filter that darkens the world view, as in waking, the dreamer is free of these elements, and is thus, undiluted peace. This is why you are happy to go back to sleep, even if your dream was mundane. The objective of this book is to help you bring the unencumbered witness of the dream into your waking life. This undiluted seer is peace. Just knowing this is a strong pointer on the path to freedom. The dropping of conditioning as an identity yields many unanticipated benefits:

- Improved impulse control
- Less neediness
- Zero process-addictions and obsessions

- Decreased physical appetites, but with no loss of enjoyment
- Cessation of unwanted thoughts, fears, and desires
- Cure of psychosomatic illness
- Reduced stress
- Better sleep and more vivid dreaming
- Improved short-term memory
- Increased energy
- Increased patience
- Less judging/blaming of others
- Increased empathy
- Happier with social life
- Happier with work
- Positive outlook

Take any one of the above benefits and fit it into the question, "what if I could _____?" Achieving even one of them in an appreciable way could be life-changing.

CHAPTER ONE
Crave New World

The opportunities to become addicted to and obsessed with things have never been greater. Technology has facilitated so many forms of entertainment, communication, and access to information, that we can constantly engage outside content. But the real source of obsession and process-addiction is in us, not the technology that exacerbates it. Our susceptibility to obsession is due to an internal imbalance. Something inside us has become ravenous, and we're desperately trying to placate it with whatever eases the pangs. However, it's hard to see the stealthy connection between the outside things and the hunger. We typically have a chance to glimpse our dependence only when the pacifier becomes a problem. Then we either address the underlying issue of the hunger or ignore it and move on to using something less disruptive, staying dependent on the new thing until it too becomes problematic. Outside things take many forms: objects, relationships, activities and substances. These four categories contain innumerable sub-categories. At the heart of it is a single theme, "seeking." We are nearly all in some way seeking. An addiction or obsession is merely a dead-end in the maze of seeking. But what isn't a dead end? Everything in the world has an expiration date, and so there is no lasting happiness to be found in things. The attractions themselves contain no joy, as they need not even change for us to stop deriving joy *from* them. It is the mind that loses interest in the object. When the newness is gone, the mind once again modulates consciousness with lower vibrations and sets the being on another quest for relief through distraction. They are merely props to pull our attention out of that which diminishes our joy, the sedimentary mind that envelops and darkens consciousness. It is built from thoughts, a balloon man full of emotional energy. To the one who saw him molded and inflated, the mind is like a voodoo doll that traps consciousness within, forcing it to take on and express the coloring of its conditioned perspectives. The construct must be protected, but it is nothing but a pile of thoughts given power by attachment and unkempt emotional energy. Obsessive thoughts have an addictive quality to them, and so breaking the addiction to addictions involves the cultivation of an ability to demagnetize your attention from thoughts.

The problem of "want" is analogous to alcohol or drug abuse in that it's trying to use something from the outside to replace something that's wrongly believed to be lacking on the inside. With drug abuse, the drug is a neurotransmitter that mimics one the body produces naturally. Eventually, the body stops producing its own neurotransmitter, and you're stuck having to outsource it through the drug, which creates health problems and interferes with life. In process addiction, there is a release of endogenous dopamine that accompanies the addictive action. Since the dopamine is produced naturally within us, it's not a part of the equation we immediately consider, but it is the hidden constant. We're using an outside stimulus to generate an endogenous drug. We're the addict. The dopamine is the drug, and the addictive activity is the dispenser. Process addiction is obvious to the partners of those who are immersed in it, but until it interferes with life multiple times, it's often masked to the sufferer. This is because the activity itself might not be inherently bad, when done in moderation. The hidden problem is the brain's habituation to this type of stimulation. A specific addictive behavior is just one drug dealer, and so it's not enough to break a specific addictive activity. There's another behavior waiting around the corner. You have to break the internal pattern of need to stop the cycle of addiction. This is an inside job.

CHAPTER TWO
Inner Space

One need not identify as a process addict to experience the frustration of trying to find fulfillment in life. The pattern of using acquisitions and experiences as a crutch to happiness is nearly universal. It is based on the way the world molds us from childhood. As we grow and age, we become more strongly identified with the body and mind. To the extent that our attention engages them, we believe them to be ourselves. But the body and mind are observed by that which animates them, and so we are missing something.

In order to sort out the inner space, we should identify the elements of the individual. There is you, which is pure consciousness or awareness, then the body, through which we sense and interact with the outside world, and then there is the mind, the individuated consciousness, as modified by experience. There are three mediums at play among the three elements: thoughts that comprise the mind, emotions, which are triggered by the mind but felt in the body, and the joy that is pure consciousness, the space of "you" that has not been adulterated by outside content, i.e., "the mind." They are interconnected in a number of ways.

The mind directs emotional energy in the body and also does problem solving. The mind is focused on maintaining the body, which is consciousness's connection to this world. It is a survival tool. Autonomic functions aside, the mind starts as a space of pure consciousness and begins to accumulate experiences into which it forms an identity. This identity, the ego, like the body, is another thing the mind seeks to defend, as the ego lives in the mind. In warfare, there is the option of having a fixed position, a base from which an army operates. A fixed position must be defended. In the inner-being, the ego is a fixed position. It can be attacked and therefore, it must be defended. The defense of the ego's positions consumes a tremendous amount of mental and emotional energy, and the prospect of its fall is a constant source of fear. It should also be noted that the ego's positions are almost always a function of perspective; meaning, most people derive their identity from circumstances that originated upstream of their birth e.g., race, religion, nationality, physical characteristics, class, etc. To the extent that these positions are arbitrary, there isn't necessarily any merit in defending them, short of pride. This should illustrate how the ego comes in from outside and defends the turf it occupies within.

Pure consciousness or awareness, the downstream observer of all thought and experience, receives two kinds of signals from the mind, one is a composite of images, memories, wishes, fears, and abstract thoughts, and the other are direct outside stimuli, which pass straight through the brain from the senses and into awareness. This latter is what we call real-world experience. We, as consciousness, don't have an interpretation of the outside world without the brain. The brain, as an organ, is like a window for consciousness, which knows unity with creation when not clouded with thought and emotion. The eyes are the "eyes" of the brain, and the brain is the eye of consciousness in this world.

The human brain is like an internal media player, translator, and editor. Its medium is thought. It receives input from the senses and translates it into thought, which it then plays back for its internal audience, you, the consciousness. Thoughts are not original to the mindspace. They are comprised of bits of information that your mind has recorded through the senses. Abstract thoughts are derived from other thoughts. The thoughts are like movies and audio tracks. You can view or listen to them or you can spend time using your mind to edit them. This is thinking, and you spend a great deal of time doing it.

Your mind is programmed by its experiences. Thinking causes it to form neural pathways that correlate to certain skills or patterns of behavior. The brain is conditioned by thought and experience, and that conditioning solidifies with age, but the brain is malleable. You can change the way you think, and if you persist in the change for long enough, it will alter the brain's neural pathways, making the new way easier for you. This is the essence of learning and unlearning. This is relevant to obsession and process-addiction in that they are both thought-based. Thought is a critical link in the addictive pattern. Altering the thought path can break the chain of addiction.

The distinction between you and your mind is a key concept. There was a time when your prefrontal-cortex was not fully-developed, and yet, you were conscious. The consciousness observes, and thus, it is you. It was there before the voice in your head came into being, before the thought player arose. The inner-space is a zero-sum game between thought and consciousness. A preponderance of thought, particularly negative thought, which takes up more space, will hamper the expansion of pure consciousness within you. Less consciousness means less joy. When you were a child, before you started thinking so much, there was more room for pure untainted consciousness. This is why a child can get joy from playing with something as mundane as a stick. By paring back the thoughts, it is possible to restore consciousness to its rightful place in your being. It's possible to regain the wonder of childhood.

CHAPTER THREE
Consciousness Versus the Mind

Pure consciousness is the joy that fills you when all of your cares are pushed aside. People confuse the thing that pushes their cares away with the joy that flows in behind it. That joy is the stillness of consciousness expanding through the inner-space. Outside things that give us a temporary mood elevation are merely "levers" that push aside our worries for a time. If you had no worries, and I mean not a care in the world, not a thought, not a grudge, not an ambition, it would create a space in you into which pure consciousness would expand, revealing the peace within. This state is similar to the inner arrangement of the child, our original state, but there's something else. There's something missing from childhood that appears in the adult, and that is the volume of negative thoughts. Children are so much more positive than adults. Negative thoughts weigh heavily on the mind and darkly cloud consciousness. Another factor is the concept of time. Time is just a way to describe our distance from a reality that is no longer available to us, and the future is just a concept, and the mind knows nothing true about it. Time is wholly of the human imagination, the mind. The five senses can apprehend nothing but reality, and it simply changes like a face. We have merely correlated the changes to the movements of celestial bodies for convenience and called it time. The future is a lie. To live in a lie is to become alienated from your Self. The child has no past from which to draw painful memories, and the future is not yet a beacon that outshines reality with glimmering promises. They just don't see far enough into the future or past to be living in deep untruth.

For one who constantly ignores now for later, the future is like the sun, brighter when there's more of it on the horizon. The adult has a lot more angst stored up in the mental past, and less bright a future than was typically imagined as a child, plus less of it. This means that the adult mind has an ever-expanding past timeline of nostalgia and regret from which to piece together a "menu" of negativity, along with a side of anxiety, compliments of the ever-shrinking future. This split landscape that lies on either side of the present is the playground of the mind. The present is the rock on which you may stand and be free of the mind, so long as you can stay wholly immersed in it, allowing the audio and visuals of the mind to be in perfect harmony with those of the moment.

Consciousness is the pristine perspective, the silent space within. You are joy when thought is absent and emotion is appropriate to the moment. Or you could look at it another way, some kinds of thoughts are bad, and you should have less of them. You're basically happy by default, but then the mind, with its thoughts, comes in, and they play up all of your anxieties and hurts. On top of that, the mind's prescription for all that ails is something "out there," a perfect relationship or that nice house and car. That's what your mind wants you to focus on. It does not want to give up any space to consciousness. The mind wants to stay active inside you. It doesn't really care about your happiness. It just wants to help you find faux happiness in outside things. Why does the mind create need in us? Like all things in our body, the mind is an evolutionary adaptation.

CHAPTER FOUR
A Theory of the Mind

Our minds are hard-wired to ever-advance our adaptive capabilities through outside things. There was a time when man lived in a circular way. There was nothing called progress. He did not have the ability or inclination to synthesize anything from the environment. Living in the circle means that ways are not abandoned unless the environment demands change. The circle accumulates nothing, and it has no need for memory because nothing on a circle can be left behind. In the absence of change, there is no nostalgia beyond the interpersonal level. Animals live in an intergenerational circle. Imagine a graph with time on the horizontal axis and adaptive capability on the vertical axis. Animals would be a straight horizontal line. Their ability to adapt does not change at all. It's based on intergenerational selection, which is dependent on conditions; therefore, the patterns of their lives vary little from one generation to the next. Humans would have started this way, and then, with the advent of tools, an unprecedented thing occurred, a positive slope on the measure of adaptive capability, and from there, the slope has sharpened. This function has a positive second derivative, an accelerating adaptive capability. We are two-levels removed from animals in that we advance at an advancing rate. Animals are static, and we are not. Man's departure from the circle began slowly but then accelerated, and we see it through recorded history, explosive population growth and technological advancement. We are on a trajectory that is no longer a circle but a line. Consider that nearly every human born in the last several hundred years has had to watch the world abandon the ways in which he/she grew up. Considering that the ego is invested in its formative experiences, this obsolescence of its lessons is tremendously threatening. It is the source of the generation gap. The mind's propensity to always seek more is what drives change. It's ironic that the actions of some minds cause others to be obsolete. This constant change is also a source of apprehension about the future. The beginning of our journey necessitated the creation of a mind. The mind is what we use to get outside things. That's the precise purpose for which it is evolved. Animals don't have a prefrontal cortex quite like ours, and therefore, they don't seek anything but that which provides for their immediate needs, even if that need is storing up food as a response to the changing of seasons. The act is hard-wired into the animal. There is no discretion in it. The human being needed a mind to get and use outside things, but it came at the expense of his consciousness. Consciousness is the joy that accompanies living in truth, which is nothing but reality, the moment. Staying apart from the mind's medium of unreality, of lies, is the true absence of cares, for the mind is evolved to ever tell you that you do not have enough. The two are mutually exclusive. How did we get here? Man once had everything in common with the rest of the universe, for it all runs in circles and cycles. Then man broke out of the circle in developing the ability to manipulate his environment. Once man could change the environment and build a body of ideas that could be passed to future generations, he left the circle and moved onto a line, which has a beginning and an end. This path brings him in contact with novelty. The circle is the bliss of apprehending what is ahead and never having to divorce what's behind. It's like living in the moment. The line is full of duality, such as the hope or dread of the future and the cherished or lamented time of the past. It perpetually faces the unknown and perpetually abandons everything it once valued. Man's mark on the universe looks like a rupture in the fabric of this realm of circular things, a rupture from which oozes the detritus of a parallel dimension that has no symmetry.

In the beginning, there was consciousness, and we were as satisfied as any living thing. Then came the mind. Humans are different because of our minds. Our prefrontal cortex gives us the ability to see the dimension of time. To animals, there is no time, only changing stimuli to which they react. Animals are perfectly balanced between mind, body, and an awareness, a consciousness. They have no need to elevate consciousness through outside things. They have virtually no "things," and yet they are content. They fit into their niches and function until the niche changes, and then they adapt, die off, or give way to a better-adapted species. Human beings do not have a balance between mind and consciousness, as the latter had to give way to the former. We decided to get out of step with creation and do it all for ourselves, trying to get everything in a proportion greater than was built into the system. We sacrificed the contentment of consciousness for the restlessness of the mind. The human mind is so powerful that its imagined scenarios are interpreted by the body as real. Since there is no limit to what the mind can imagine, it subjects the body to unnecessary stress from a variety of imagined things. How did man get so unique a thing as this blessing and curse that is the mind? I believe that somehow the primacy of the human mind stems from a single, original thought, which was essentially, "I know better." The pre-human was in his niche, but then he found a way to get more of what he needed by doing something different. The first human left his ecological niche during his own lifetime. Intra-lifespan adaptation is unique to man. Animal species can move from one niche to another, but it takes many generations of selection to make that jump. The human learned how to use an outside thing to get more of what he wanted. And what happened as a result? We needed more outside things. Our ability to use tools brought us into new environments that called for even further adaptation, which meant even more outside things. Eventually, the environments we inhabited were so far removed from the original human niche, that to not have outside things meant certain death. This is exacerbated by the fact that with each outside thing we mastered, it replaced a capability we acquired through selection, e.g., fur, nails, and agility, leaving us dependent on the outside thing, the definition of addiction. Now that we've learned how to replace our environment with one that suits our debilitated bodies, we're losing the environment, as in the natural world, as well. In summary, we have a mind that is adapted to create want. Your mind believes that if it doesn't keep you wanting more outside things, it will die in the face of unending change. In order to be content, you must power down the seeker, the means that calls itself an end, and live as its observer and master, the consciousness that once believed it. It is possible to stimulate a remapping of neural pathways to   do   exactly   this.

CHAPTER FIVE
Framing the Problem

Heartache, obsession, and process-addiction have a common element among them, thought. Thought is a product of the mind, which controls the body, both directly through willful movement and indirectly through emotions, which trigger physiological responses. The mind colors the expression of consciousness. Your inability to stop doing or thinking something is a function of several complex internal processes, including thoughts and the release of hormones and neurotransmitters, but thought is a limiting factor that lies upstream of them all. In the case of heartache, you just can't stop thinking of your lost love, and that thought triggers an emotional response, releasing stress hormones. The emotion and chemicals released in your body make you feel sad.

When you're caught in process-addiction, your mind constantly wanders back to the addictive action. Merely thinking of it will elevate your mood, and then carrying it out gives you an even greater boost. Underlying both thought and action are the need to elevate consciousness. The thought is the trigger, but it also plays a larger and less-acknowledged role as the "agent of lack" relative to consciousness. Thought crowds out consciousness.

The need to elevate consciousness through outside means is due to something lacking inside. Engaging in addictive behavior gives you a feeling of full awareness. The temporary boost in consciousness is characterized by a "pushing out" of negative thoughts and feelings. When you're doing "your thing," it dissolves your stresses and cares, replacing them with pure consciousness that flows into your being. Pure consciousness is the joy that accompanies having not a care in the world. It is you, a joy now palpable in your frame. Its presence is automatic in the absence of troubles, both real and imagined. Decreasing the volume of unnecessary thoughts at play reduces the number of potential "triggers" for the addictive action, and it also reduces the amount of care and worry in your mind, which makes room for consciousness.

The process addict has a lack of internal space for consciousness stemming from an overabundance of thought, which precipitates negative emotions and stress. He/she has to use the addictive behavior as a lever to temporarily "push back" the internal clutter, so that consciousness may enter and bring joy. Unfortunately, the mind gets used to the "lever" over time, and a greater volume and/or intensity of the behavior is needed to provide the same relief. This is actually true for most people, hence consumerism, but the process addict is a more extreme case.

A typical person has a balance of silence, thought, and emotion that is a function of the outside balance of his or her life. They may still be subject to the whims of the mind but are maintaining a balance of external pacifiers that allows them to be stable and functional. However, if one or two of these pacifiers is thrown off or they experience an event that plunges them into the depths of despair, they will either seek an outside thing for consolation or become a seeker of the inner-solution. There is the chance for freedom if the mind becomes so offensive that it is noticed as the root of emotional turbulence. In ignoring the call of the mind's alternatives and instead, surrendering to the emotions that underlie resistance to "what is," feeling them, and letting them go, the mind will begin to deflate, leaving a gap between it and its observer. This gap is one of pure consciousness that provides relief. In the continued practice of surrender and presence, staying faithful to the moment, this quiet space will expand, revealing its peace. In time, it is realized that one is neither form, nor conditioning, nor circumstance, nor position, and in dropping loyalty to these arbitrary things that are observed, their witness becomes liberated. You almost have to find this solution by accident, by grace.

CHAPTER SIX
Stressful's Not Restful

Humans have a realm of imagination not present in animals. As three-dimensional beings, both humans and animals can experience only one moment at a time, as it arises. There is no fast forward or reverse. However, the human brain has a concept of the future and past, and animal brains do not. The mind is evolved to protect you from all dangers, immediate and anticipated, but your immediate surroundings rarely contain a true threat, and therefore, the mind sets to work on identifying all the potential dangers that can be extrapolated from your life-circumstances. Once a potential problem is identified, the mind springs forth to attack it. It creates a simulation of the problem and a projection of the protagonist (you) doing battle with it, running through every scenario to find the path to victory. The problem with this exercise is that your body reads all this mind-generated stimulation as if it were real, and so the nervous system generates numerous physiological responses through fear, anxiety, anger, and any number of other negative emotions. This behavior on the part of the mind damages the body through the production of stress hormones and radiates harm outward in the form of emotional transference. The buildup of negative emotional energy seeks release, and thus, small annoyances can trigger outsized responses. Like an attack dog, if you let it get away from you, the mind will find something to fight. The more room you give it to run into its concept of the future, the bigger the imaginary opponents it will find. So for example, if you just let it run to tomorrow, it will probably think of something you have to do at work, no big deal. However, if you let it run out a couple of years, it could be thinking about an illness, the death of a loved one, losing your job, a major war or economic collapse. The possible foes are limitless, and the problem with letting your mind get out this far into the future is that the larger the opponent, the harder it is to call it back into reality. Keep your mind in the present if you want to have a happy life.

If your brain were more primitive, you would have no option with respect to where your attention could be. It would have to be in the here and now. The problem with the human brain's ability to put itself into a concept of the past and future manifests in terms of its effects on the rest of the person. The mind is the director of the body, and so its imaginary scenarios create physical responses. Think about something stressful or unpleasant, and your body will respond to it in any number of ways, e.g., sweating, increased heart rate, shaking, crying, etc. When an animal's biological needs are met, it can rest and be content. Its rest is more rejuvenating than that of most humans, because for an animal, when there is no external stimulation, there is little-to-no internal stimulation. Human rest is only partial-rest in that even when the body is not dealing with the stresses of external stimuli, it could be bombarded with imaginary scenarios from the brain, causing physical stress. This is a non-trivial difference that uniquely impacts our species' ability to feel contentment.

However, it is possible to train your mind to avoid this kind of stress.

CHAPTER SEVEN
How Daydreams Ruin Your Day

The human being, unique among animals by virtue of his brain, is subject to stimulation that goes beyond that which arises from external stimuli in the present. The consequences go beyond just the amount of stress that's put on the body. There is also a diminishing of the perceived vibrance of life. Think of a real, present-moment experience as being a meal. If it's a good meal, you derive a certain satisfaction and enjoyment from it. However, if you haven't eaten very much that day, you will enjoy it even more. But isn't the opposite also true? What if it's a good meal, but you've been eating junk food all day? The meal wouldn't be as good. You might not even finish it. The constant saturation of consciousness with thought is like ruining your appetite with junk food. Our mundane lives don't compare with the quick fix offered by daydreams. Have you ever bought a lottery ticket and fantasized about winning? Fantasies are somewhat like junk food in that they are easy to devour. They give us a quick mental high, but then reality sets in, and we have a bit of a "comedown," the minor disappointment you feel when your lottery ticket doesn't win. Going back to your normal life makes it feel less gratifying when you've been dreaming of easy money.

If idle thought is junk food, reality is a wholesome meal. The mental junk food you take in and digest through rumination, even while at rest, is going to diminish the satisfaction you get from the real-world experience. Thoughts and reality satisfy the same appetite because consciousness resonates with both thought and true, external sense data. You are the one who observes reality, and you are the one who observes thoughts. The thought and reality "data-feeds" play out on the same screen, consciousness and bodily form. Stop thinking so much and your real-world experience will be more enjoyable.

CHAPTER EIGHT
Planning or Fretting?

Compare the case of a blind date to that of meeting someone spontaneously. We conjure up images of our date based on the outcome we want. When the person doesn't live up to our expectations, it seems natural to feel some disappointment. However, what if we met that same person spontaneously and with no pretext for potential dating? All things being equal, do we feel any disappointment when we unexpectedly make an acquaintance and they happen to not be "our-type," romantically? No, and it's because we dealt with the situation as it arose, there was no time for the mind to ruin it with anxiety and expectations.

Another example would be going to the doctor or dentist. I personally don't care to visit either, and I used to dread the days leading up to an appointment. My mind was looking into the future and dropping stress on me in the present. Aside from death and grievous injury, stress is the worst thing we get from an unwanted bodily experience. Physical pain is just a symptom of something else. It's an alarm. The pain itself doesn't cause the damage. Stress is different. Stress has a pain element to it, but it also inflicts damage on the body in the release of stress hormones. So when my mind jumps ahead to a trouble that could potentially happen in the future, I'm suffering stress to no good end. It increases the cumulative pain of an event, and with no benefit. The irony is that the event might never occur, and there's no limit to the number of phantom events that your mind can create and stress over. Assuming we're not talking about serious bodily harm, the physical pain of an event is far less consequential than the stress leading up to it. The same holds true for memories, the other side of the timeline. Lamenting the past is like making mortgage payments on a house you can't live in.

A mind that is allowed to wander into the future will invariably find problems that generate stress and anxiety. I would liken such stress to paying interest. In personal finance, if you had the ability to pay for all non-appreciating assets in cash, it would save you the cost of interest, and you would thus, be more wealthy. So by the same token, if you deal with every anticipated problem just when it occurs, without a care for it in advance, it would spare you a great deal of stress, which would improve your life in unexpected ways. There's nothing wrong with identifying problems and preparing to deal with them, when they arise. If you can do that while at the same time keeping your mind from "pre-visiting" them outside of legitimate planning, you will be as stress-free as the dog, who doesn't know he's going to the vet until he's in the parking lot. You may even best the dog in not having any stress until the moment you feel the pinch of the needle. You kept your mind quiet and so the topic of the doctor's appointment never came up inside it. This is how it is for a person whose mind has been trained to not unnecessarily jump ahead.

CHAPTER NINE
Too Much Thinking

Now consider that there is something inside of you that calls for stimulation and novelty. We all have this need. It's why solitary confinement can lead to madness. We receive stimulation from a blend of internal thoughts and external reality, and our level of happiness can vary with the proportions of each that we receive in the blended signal. A person in solitary confinement feels that they are blocked off from the external signal, and so the internal signal predominates, which can lead to madness.

The amount of stimulation we need to combat boredom is a function of the level of excitement to which we've become accustomed. This explains the letdown you feel when returning to normal life after an exciting and adventurous vacation, a hangover of sorts. The historical level of input sets the baseline for what's required to get additional gratification. Given that your brain exposes you to extra stimulation via thoughts, your threshold for a satisfactory level of excitement is significantly higher than that of an animal or a small child, whose stimulation is limited to dealing with only what it can immediately sense. "Simple minds are easily amused," but jaded minds need to up the ante. Staying in the moment helps shrink the appetite for novelty and thus increases the appreciation of all things novel.

The world of worries and dreams is rarely about average things. It's more often the best or worst. Thoughts are not bound by limits, and so they can be spectacular or horrific. Reality is more stable. You can calm your inner being by decreasing the number of thoughts flowing through consciousness. The expanded bandwidth that gets devoted to reality smooths the extreme swings. Imagine thought as a sine wave. It has extreme highs and lows. You can average the signal down by adding more reality, which is smoother. Try to get by with as little unnecessary thinking as possible and see what happens.

In the early 1800's, William Wordsworth composed the poem, "The World is too Much With Us," and the world has indeed become considerably more distracting and engrossing than it was even thirty years prior to this writing. If you doubt that, consider how many passwords you must manage today, understanding that in the 1980's, passwords were more frequently encountered in spy novels than in the real world. The increased complexity of life has added stress, and technology has provided so much instant gratification that the lack of waiting has atrophied our patience. There has also been an intensification of the content that the media provides. If you were born in the 1970's or before, you've likely witnessed the progression of sex and violence that's portrayed on television. The circus no longer entertains us, and so we've made circuses of our lives. The world is crowding consciousness, even as it promises to bestow the same on machines. Therefore, it is imperative that you guard the senses. There can be no peace if the senses constantly engage what is essentially, an externalized mind in the form of the media stream, e.g., social media, news, entertainment, etc. These sources of mental stimulation are much like thought in that they require little work to mentally digest. They are mental junk food that increases your appetite for stimulation. But what's worse, since they come from places of profit motive, they are manipulative. They are specifically and carefully designed and edited to both attract your attention, to sell advertising, as well as cultivate fear and a sense of separation to stimulate consumption in the pursuit of security. Even if their source is a private individual, there are algorithms that point you to them, based on your browsing history. They take you down the rabbit hole in the same way as the mind. Bad news and identity politics bolster the veil that hides the spiritual heart and gives a false and vulnerable reflection of self to its witness. In doing so, they generate fear and hate. In the aggregate, people do not change, and yet, their group behavior changes over time. Why is this? It's because we are conditioned beings, and whoever controls the media content controls the conditioning. There has been no evolutionary shift in man that has precipitated the increase in suicides and mass shootings in the decades leading up to the time of this book's writing, it's the content we're being fed and our tendency to engage it. Wean yourself from the media products of other hungry minds. Guard your senses by cutting out social media, video surfing, and news. They are all provided by monied interests that profit from human unconsciousness.

Worldly stressors increase the volume of input from both the outside world and the inner-world created by the mind. We do not control the outside world, and so that is a constant in the equation, but we can theoretically control our minds. It would logically follow then, that if you could decrease the excess stimulation created by your mind, you could increase your level of happiness. That is to say, that decreasing your overall intake of stimulation by "quieting the mind," will make you less jaded, less stressed, and thus, more energetic and much more satisfied with the conditions of your life. This is how the benefit of quieting the mind accrues to those who meditate. Even meditating ten minutes in the morning and ten minutes before bed each day could change your life.

People who think too much "zone out" and live in their own imaginary world. They don't even realize they are partially in a dream world because it mimics the real world but with the addition of a mind-generated narrative that weaves it together based on their perspective, their conditioning. It's an image of the real world as they imagine it. The only way to see it otherwise is to set aside all of your positions. If your happiness relative to life-circumstance decreases with the amount of ruminating and worrying you do, then those who spend the most time in their heads should exhibit lower happiness and a greater tendency toward addiction. Their minds exaggerate troubles and inflate expectations.

CHAPTER TEN
Why We Seek, and Why We Shouldn't

A spiritual friend once asked me what differentiates man from beast, and I fumbled for an answer, talking about science and art, but now it occurs to me that wild animals do not have an inner void to fill. They experience reality in a way that is significantly different than humans because they lack a highly developed prefrontal-cortex.

Animals simply don't have a human mind. The hardware's missing. This means they take direction exclusively from here and now. Their lack of a higher brain gives them the luxury of having to deal with the present-only. The human being is subject to a different internal order in that the mind knows how to confront us with multiple issues from various points along the timeline. Most of our problems are in our minds, and as such, there is no limiting factor on how many of them can be conjured up. The mind is ever-creating imaginary problems which constantly need fixing through distraction, which is in turn, the reason why many of us constantly need something from outside of ourselves to fix them. Our finite world might not survive our species' attempt to satiate its infinite, imaginary needs. We have to find a way to satisfy ourselves that does not entail stripping the planet bare in the attempt.

There is an insatiable hunger in man that is a function of his inability to recognize what satisfies it. Consider what a lion does when its biological needs are met. It's generally content to do nothing. It lays there and observes or sleeps. It needs nothing more.

It doesn't worry about getting a freezer to store up more meat. It doesn't worry about some problem that has yet to manifest. It doesn't need to get things to address problems because it has no problems. For man or beast, contentment is the natural state in the absence of problems, real or imagined. The difference between the human and lion is that the lion's perception of problems is aligned with reality and the human's is not. When the lion looks through the window of his inner being, he sees right now. There is nothing out there to threaten him. If something arises, he will deal with it at that moment. The human can look at the same reality, but it will be through the prism of his mind, and even if there's no problem in the present, the mind will create one and project it to him. Phantom problems can motivate real-world action, but if we, at the individual level, can separate ourselves from the mind's untruths, we'll be content as the lion. Otherwise, we are drawing on finite resources to address imaginary and thus, infinite problems. It's clear that we collectively are in a terminal game of whack-a-mole. We're trying to fill a hole with something that won't fill it.

CHAPTER ELEVEN
The Role of Emotional Energy

The realm of emotions is associated with the body. Emotion is a utility that's adapted to direct energy within the body for the survival of the individual and species. Emotions cause physical reactions. When you're angry or frightened, your heart rate jumps and you feel the blood surge from your extremities into your core. This is to enhance your survival chances in the event of a grievous injury. When you are sad, you weep and your body produces tears. Emotions create powerful waves of feeling that have bodily consequences. You can die from fright. Emotions arise due to two forms of stimuli, thought, and input from the senses. Most emotion comes from thoughts of an imagined reality, e.g., the past, and not true reality, as in right now. If you could limit the emotions to that which arose from the immediate, without a thought for the past, you would have a lot less negativity and stress, which would make you feel less compelled to elevate your consciousness through outside means.

The emotional reaction to stimuli will draw energy from the body to bring about the physiological changes most conducive to survival in a particular range of situations, but given that our modern world is relatively new to us in evolutionary terms, our bodies are adapted to more treacherous times than today. The human body is evolved to give the amount of energy required to overcome a situation, as there is no "tie" or compromise in nature. It's win or go extinct. Our bodies react as if everything is "win

43

or die." It's true that the reaction is proportional to the magnitude of the event, but most emotional reactions today will be over-reactions, because we come from a line of progenitors who won the survival game every single time in a more brutal world. Only those who put forth at least enough energy to survive passed on their genes. If they overreacted to situations, they could be imperiled as well, due to stress. Our emotional response is right-sized for the paleolithic but outsized for the modern world. As a species having only recently attained the ability to create an environment that minimizes our exposure to mortal danger, we have a "fast idle," more energy directed towards primitive ends than is needed. Our nervous system is behind the times.

Life in the paleolithic was rough and short. The number and average magnitude of physically-dangerous situations we encounter has declined since then. However, the number of threatening situations has increased dramatically. To our stone-aged body, all threats are mortal danger, as this was the case for the majority of our evolutionary incubation. To have a dispute with your neighbors in the stone-age could have resulted in exile or death. Unfortunately, we're not yet evolved to properly handle a large number of threatening, but not-necessarily-deadly situations. For example, going for a drive can produce a huge number of emotional micro-events. The same goes for the modern workplace.

Every time we have a stressor, our body produces an emotional charge, which is partially expended by the event, but depending on its magnitude relative to the reaction, there could be a significant residual of unspent emotional energy, stress. Newton's law of there being for every action, an equal and opposite reaction, applies to emotions as well as motion. When excess emotional energy goes stale and turns into stress, it's a residual that needs to be eliminated. Stress is like an emotional fat cell that gets stored away. When you don't dissipate your emotional energy, it accumulates, and that eventually gives rise to negative thoughts, which can themselves stir up more emotion and stress. The mind is energized by emotion, which precipitates thought, which crowds out consciousness, which precludes joy. Thoughts are given the power to inflict pain through negative emotional energy. The goal of what follows is to instruct in the managing of emotional energy for the purpose of eliminating unwanted thoughts.

The source of the excess emotional energy is the overhang that occurs when our stone-aged body overreacts to our frequent, but not life-threatening modern problems. We hang onto a bit of the situation and carry it with us. We return to it for rumination, and then it becomes a bus stop of the mind. Just as the modern world has us eating more calories than we can burn, it also has us generating more emotional energy than we can spend through the body alone. This excess emotional energy contributes to the overstimulation of the mind, which converts the raw emotional energy into negative, emotionally-charged thoughts.

The purpose of managing your emotional energy is to prevent its accumulation, which awakens and fuels negative thoughts. Emotional energy is something that you can physically feel. An extreme case would be when you have a fright or observe something that causes you to "well up" with tears. You can identify emotional energy as a feeling you get in the area of your solar plexus. An extremely positive example of this would be the "butterflies" you feel at the thought of someone with whom you're infatuated. A negative example of this would be the way you feel when you've driven half-a-block before you realize that you've left your phone in a public place. You immediately feel that in the core of your body. If you focus on this area, you can sometimes "feel" emotional energy that has built up. I want you to try to cultivate an ongoing awareness of the emotional energy inside you. There is a correlation between its buildup and the eventual need to spend it.

In the case of compulsive and emotionally-charged thoughts or obsessions, the mind will link the energy up with the thought, which can cause a great deal of pain.

CHAPTER TWELVE
An Emotional Powerhouse

Imagine that your whole being is a dwelling. The window on that dwelling is your body, through which you sense the world. You are the consciousness, the one who observes it all, the house's first occupant, ahead of the mind. Beyond the window is the world of the present. As you grew, the mind came into your house. The mind is analogous to a computer in that it helps you process information and store it for later.

When you were young, the computer was accumulating mostly practical programs, like speech and the names of colors, how to put on clothes and properly use the bathroom. You were taking in useful information and recalling it for productive use. The computer was too new to have accumulated a lot of autobiographical programs, such as the analysis of emotionally-charged memories. It also didn't have a concept of the future or death. If there were thoughts of the future, they were pleasant ones because you had no responsibilities. This means that your inner-space was not clouded with emotionally-charged and stressful thoughts. This allowed your consciousness to take in the wonder of life without the input being polluted by the upstream negativity of grown-up cares. The problem with the computer in our metaphorical house is that it eventually competes for attention with the reality of the outside world. The problems it conjures up seem increasingly important as we grow and take on responsibilities. Simultaneous immersion in both the mind and reality is not possible. Teachers know this in dealing with children who daydream. You cannot fully bask in the light of reality if you're giving attention to the programs of the mind.

The computer of the mind also requires emotional energy to run certain programs. Emotional energy could be likened to the electricity in the house. Thoughts are the programs, and they have different functions, features, and "system requirements." Practical, task-oriented thoughts, like a recipe, take up almost no emotional energy and don't distract you when you're not using them. They can also be easily turned on and off. The thought of how peel a banana is not likely going get stuck looping in your mind. Other thoughts, obsessions, are more like malware; they pull consciousness in as if metal to magnate, hijack your attention and immerse it completely in the mind. These thoughts can also hack into the emotional power grid and steal power. They are the worst memories and fears that you can conjure up. They sap so much emotional energy that they leave you physically drained. They transmute emotional energy into negative emotions, which in turn can feed other thoughts. They release emotions like anger, guilt, grief, fear, regret, longing, self-righteous pride, etc.

Negative thoughts cause pain by stirring up the emotions. Emotional reactions are not consistent, even in the same person. A lot of how we react to something has to do with what's happening on the inside at the time. If we have pent up emotion, it is going to find a way to express itself. Negative, emotionally-charged thoughts will arise, and the more emotional energy you've stored up, the more painful the thoughts will be. Negative thoughts seem to arise from the cistern of residual emotional energy. A concrete example of this would be transference. You have a frustrating day at work and come home full of negative thoughts and pent-up emotional energy. Then someone has an accident or bad news, and you explode on them, unleashing the whole day's accumulation of negative emotion on a relative bystander. They accidentally tapped into what you neglected to manage. In order to prevent this, you must practice emotional power management. Negative thoughts arise from residual emotional energy like mosquitos from stagnant water. As with mosquitos, you can decrease the problem by taking away the breeding ground. This practice is the first step in stopping the cycle of unwanted wants, the first step in yanking the starter out of the obsession/addiction engine.

CHAPTER THIRTEEN
You Can't Wrestle a Grizzly

When negative emotional energy suddenly arises from a thought or event or it accumulates to the point where you can feel it in your solar plexus, it needs to be addressed. Every so often, when in a safe and comfortable place, close your eyes, relax your muscles from head-to-toe and focus your attention on the area of your solar plexus. Breathe and feel your breathing. Emotional energy is more-easily felt on the bottom of the exhale. Exhale slowly, and when you reach the bottom, focus on the area between the breast and belly button. Emotional energy is felt like a tingle here. When you can actually feel that energy, you can dissipate it by feeling it, focusing on it, and then embracing it and letting it make you feel however it makes you feel. Do not resist how it makes you feel, and do not react to it. You are not identifying or engaging any thoughts here. You are embracing raw emotions and feeling them fully so that they may dissipate. Even if the mind has already converted the energy into a thought, it's still possible to gain immediate relief through this practice. Whatever the negative thought is, it has an underlying negative emotion, e.g., sorrow, fear, anger, guilt, grief, self-righteous pride, vindication in being the victim, etc., and you can surrender to the emotion without even focusing on the thought it fed. You are relaxed on the inside for this whole time, as if the emotion is trying to carry you away, and yet you go dead limp to it, making it carry your full weight until it runs out of energy and lets you go.

It is essential that every time you feel negative emotional energy rising in you, you immediately turn your attention to it, and carry out the steps mentioned above. Think of negative emotional energy as a Grizzly Bear. Every time he comes around, you have a choice; you can fight him or play dead. Nobody beats the Grizzly. He just eats you and gets stronger. You can only win by going limp to it, as if to say, "you can eat me if you want, but I'm betting you'll go away if I just lay here." Doing this with dedication will stop the negative thoughts in you. It will make you feel like you've unloaded a heavy burden. Do this every day, every time you feel negative emotional energy or have a negative thought, and you will feel a huge difference. It's key to do this for both unwanted thoughts of the past and present-moment situations that create unwanted emotions. If a powerful and negatively-charged memory presents itself to consciousness, and the being embraces the underlying emotion without dipping into the thought, it's like the thought was a latex balloon and the emotion was the air. The allowing of feeling facilitated the deflation of the thought. The beauty is that the next time the memory attempts to get attention, its pull will be weaker.

CHAPTER FOURTEEN
The Mind's Mischief

In conjunction with the draining of the negative emotional energy pool outlined in the previous chapters, one should not let up on quieting the mind. For a lack of emotional fuel, it will weaken and deflate to the point where consciousness will begin to notice its ebb, which will help dispel the illusion that the mind is the self. It is not. The mind/ego is a composite being built from two components. Firstly, it is an accumulation of thoughts that form a unique fingerprint of identity. These thoughts pertain to the origins of the being and the beliefs that were put into it by family and society. The mind will favor that which overlaps its fingerprint, i.e., those with whom it has things in common, such as race, origin, culture, religion, taste, age, etc. The second part of the mind/ego is the emotional energy pool that fuels it. The practice of surrender from the previous chapter is a critical part of "de-fanging" the mind. The emotional energy pool is built from residuals of emotional experiences of which we cannot let go. This is why it's so important to let the emotions pass, as not doing so quietly leaves fuel for the mind's attacks. In the unhappy individual, the mind has gone beyond its optimal scope of duties. It really is just for practical matters. It should not be allowed to pull emotional levers and torture consciousness with its grudges and fearful hypothetical scenarios. The mind will always have this bag of fears, nostalgia, regrets, and notions of separateness. It's whether or not you engage this content that determines your level of inner-peace. And to that end, the practice of surrender undercuts the emotional power supply that "magnetizes" those thoughts relative to your attention. The more static emotional energy that's allowed to reside in you, the more power the electromagnet of the mind has to pull consciousness down into its hell. If you want to stop thinking about something, it is much easier when the mind is not plugged into a massive pool of residual emotional energy.

Before your mind could form thoughts and play with words, consciousness was observing, and the emotions were actively interfacing with your parents to signal for the provision of your body. The mind is a decisioning tool that sorts through thoughts and ranks them based on its own priorities. The mind's priorities are survival of the individual and the maintenance of its imaginary position as the identity.

The mind is mute at first, having no material from which to work. As a baby, you were out of balance internally, plenty of consciousness and emotion, but no mind; however, your parents propped up the "mind" leg of the stool for you, which kept you alive until you developed a mind of your own. When you were a baby, your emotions took orders from only one master, sensory input. Because there is no mind to play thoughts that occupy inner space, the baby's internal state is one of pure consciousness, punctuated by bouts of emotion that arise and therefore dissipate, on an "as-needed basis." When all is comfortable for the infant, it is content. This is the state of the child until they begin thinking.

The baby is an interesting case because it is an example of a human with an extreme imbalance in the triad of consciousness, emotion, and thought. However, because the deficient leg of the stool is thought, which is normally trying to be the master of the other two, we can see emotion and consciousness in isolation, which is instructive. When the needs are met, there is no need for emotion, which is summoned to address a need of any kind. There is only contentment and discomfort. Back and forth it goes between the two, and the parents serve as the "mind" for the infant. So let's take what we learned here and apply it to an adult. As you grew from a child to an adult, you went from having only two legs of the stool, emotion and consciousness, to again having only two legs of the stool, emotion and mind. Consciousness receded as the mind grew. Recall that consciousness is the unconditioned awareness, the blank "space" through which movements create the appearance of both thoughts and forms, i.e., the subtle and gross reality observed by the unmanifested consciousness from which they arise. So we know from the baby that when there is a deficiency in one of the legs of the stool, the emotions become active to motivate the person to do something about it. With the baby, there is crying, and the parents come help. With the adult, there is acting out on a larger scale, and instead of summoning the parents, they're summoning an elevation of consciousness through outside things. So in the absence of any leg of the stool, the being seeks outside things to supplement. However, we all have the opportunity to have three properly functioning legs of the stool at once. We need only let go of all thought that has nothing to do with now. We must turn our attention on itself, to bring thoughts back to their source, the spiritual heart. It's when the mind has been relegated to the practical that un-manifested consciousness will become the apparent witness, the original and uncolored seer. Its unchanging aspect sees the changeful that arises from itself, and in this recognition, surrenders to its perfect unfolding. True acceptance of the perfection of all precludes the resistance of which troubling illusions are born. Meditation plays a significant role in discovering this. When stillness of consciousness expands into the space left in the resolving of the movement of mind, the reflection of its witness is unconditional peace, a reflection of love from the spiritual heart that appears in the absence of mind. It was always there but coming forth only when novelty brought alignment between the mind and the moment. With no mind to distort it, no object or circumstance is needed to still consciousness.

The mind, when properly managed, will think when needed but will otherwise be quiet. In a conscious individual, the mind fulfills its job as a survival tool, a critical function. It is a bare intelligence in the realization of its innocence. However, beyond facilitating survival, it, as a movement in consciousness born of resistance, tends to expand to be first among equals within the being. The mind crowds out pure consciousness by flooding the inner space with incessantly chattering thoughts, disturbances that yield a false reflection of self to their witness. All this mental activity takes energy, and for that, the mind turns to the triggering of emotions via certain thoughts and memories.

Thoughts are mental debris we pick up from the world. I would put thoughts into two categories practical (or utility) and discretionary. Practical thoughts could be broadly defined as survival skills, the things you need to know to live. Discretionary thoughts are personal thoughts. They are opinions and preferences, the internal narratives about you and the people in your life. They are memories, fantasies, hopes, dreams and fears. They are built from the outside world, and they are not always positive. In fact, some are quite negative and damaging, and almost all discretionary thoughts have some negative aspect to them. Even if you're thinking of a good memory, it could create longing. Looking forward to something can cause restlessness, which keeps you from enjoying the moment you're in. You could also have fear that your hopes will not be realized. Unless you're using your mind to create an actual plan or to intellectually analyze something from the past, it's healthier to keep your mind quiet. You should have your mind on a curfew. It can only go out and play in "right now," not tomorrow or yesterday.

Pure consciousness is innocent, not evolved to discern lies from truth. It is like a small child who will put inedible things in his mouth; it will pick up whatever thoughts it finds lying around. This is why people will adopt whatever worldview was imposed on them as a child, however malignant it may be. Some thoughts are rational, objects of utility, i.e., useful pieces of information that help us get around in the world. They tell us how things are done and what things are called. They are functional and typically neutral from an emotional standpoint. They seem to have no will of their own in that they lay dormant until recalled for use. It's not likely that the thought of how to change the oil in your car is going to spring to life and give you insomnia, assuming it's not correlated with another thought that gives it an emotional charge.

A neglected inner-space will be occupied by a chattering mind, overgrown with wild and ever-mutating thoughts. The untended mind will send its host on perpetual and ultimately fruitless treasure hunts for fulfillment. However, when the mind has been put in its proper place, consciousness is given space to fill. The state of pure consciousness is peace, being itself love. It's like going from battery-power to a fixed power source. Battery-power necessitates the acquisition of outside things from which to draw energy, but being able to "plug into" a permanent power source eliminates that need. Consciousness is the permanent source of fulfillment, and all outside things are temporary like batteries. Quieting the mind gives consciousness room to expand and fill you with joy. Being full of consciousness stops the drive to find happiness in outside things. When you're intrinsically happy, the consciousness that fills you shines out into the world. You put forth your best self, and it attracts good things. When the opposite is true, when you are darkened by the mind and need a "fix" to raise your spirits, you project need, which attracts more need.

Another way to think of our inner-being is like a plant. You can grow a plant from real sunlight or artificial light; however, in using artificial light, you have to pay attention to the type of bulb you use. Whereas the sun gives the perfect spectrum for plant growth, some lightbulbs are not ideal for plants. I would liken real-world stimuli to sunlight and mind-generated stimuli to light from a bulb that doesn't provide the spectrum for plant growth. The mind isn't real. A plant that doesn't get enough useful light will stretch itself thin, going upward in search of light. Like us, it hungers for something, but it's chasing the wrong kind of light. In our case, the wrong kind of light crowds out the nourishing light of reality.

The voice in your head isn't you. If it is us then most of us are internally out of control. Who can control the content of their thoughts or even when they will arise? Who can perpetually control the mental voice? There are moments when one can "grab the microphone" and control it, but then there are other times when what's heard in the mind seemingly cannot be controlled or halted. This is because there are present thoughts and speculative thoughts. Present thoughts relate only to the moment you're in, even if at this moment, it's time to make a plan. Speculative thoughts arise from the mind as reimaginings of the past or hypothetical versions of the future. Your focus should be learning how to let go of the speculative thoughts. They are rogue thoughts, like songs you've heard that keep playing in your head, but they are not you. If all you heard in life were songs, and so all that ever ran through your mind were songs, would it make sense for you to say that you, a living being, are merely a bunch of songs?

These thoughts that identify themselves as you, they are not native to you. Consciousness, the native life force in you, predates thought.

When a person is absorbed in their own mind, what passes itself off as the self is just a mass of thoughts that has taken up the inner space. Thoughts are building blocks of the false-self, some thoughts convey upon us unique status, such as victim, villain or hero. The false-self is a pile of thoughts we wear like garments to project an image to the world or the mirror. If you ask a person who they are, their explanation will often be a function of their accumulated experiences, which are from the past, and therefore, exist in the mind-only. They identify as something that is derived from that which is dead, the past. Your essence is something deeper than experience. An identity built from experiences can be changed by experience, but the pure consciousness that bore witness to the experience does not change. Experience can only be recounted as thought. Thoughts are reflections that announce an identity, but unconditioned consciousness was there first, and therefore, you are not thought. To find this, you must surrender the resistances that draw attention to thoughts of desired alternatives to what is. If we look at a computer, and you ask me what it is, I will say it's a computer, not the software that's been loaded onto it. We could erase that software, and you would still have a computer. We can load new software, and it is not a new computer. This is why people are so inconsistent, because they identify as the contents of their mind, which continuously change with experience.

The mind is a deceptive and yet unconscious thing. Its apparent life comes from the power of our attention, but it's nothing more than data, like a virus, that by itself, lacks a critical component required for life. It announces that happiness is "out there," some other place, some other time, in some outside thing, and with its help, you're going to find that happiness. The ironic truth is this, the very voice that's directing the search for happiness is the one that would die if you were to ever truly find it. No, the mind does not want to give ground to consciousness. This is because the mind itself is just a movement, and pure consciousness is the stilling of it. The true happiness is in the unconditional stilling of that movement, which the mind represents as death. Cultivating an appetite for externally-sourced happiness is a wicked device of the mind.

Negative thoughts gain an emotional charge by representing a threat or regret. Threats are of the future and regrets are of the past. They stir up emotional energy in us and feed on it, which causes them to grow and occupy space in our mind. When it comes to thoughts, the mind is like an arms dealer who sells to both sides. It profits no matter who wins. The mind loves an internal thought battle to keep itself as the center of attention. It generates thoughts that trigger an emotional response, and then it will create other thoughts to oppose or resolve the emotionally-charged thoughts it just summoned. There are any number of thoughts the mind can play to conjure up emotions. You don't know how to stop it because the only actors in the mind are thoughts themselves, and so you're fighting thoughts with other thoughts, and this swarm of thoughts just blocks out any connection to the real you, as you succumb to their incessant chatter. The thought swarm taps your energy and keeps you in a negative, noisy place, alienated from the consciousness that predates all of these interloping thoughts. Each negative thought eats up emotional energy and then excretes negative feelings, creating little fires of anger, fear, pride and regret, etc. This very likely describes the typical "inner-dialogue" of many people.

Obsession arises when an emotionally powerful thought is granted staying-power by virtue of its associations with many other thoughts. It's like a hurtful experience that's relived every time we hear that song or smell that perfume. The mobility of the negative thought is a function of the number of emotionally-neutral thoughts with which it's associated. These are "trigger thoughts," and appear as valuable or at least innocent-looking mental objects until we pick them up an find that they're wired to an emotional landmine. For example, you think of your first car, which seems a pleasant memory, but then the thought turns to how your first girlfriend dumped you for a guy who had a better car. When your mind walks the past, it's crossing a minefield of interconnected thoughts, some of which appear safe, but are wired to other more hurtful thoughts.

A thought isn't quite a living thing, but it has many similar characteristics. It's like a parasite in that you become a part of its life cycle. It entered you, lives in and gets expressed through you, and that expression gives it the opportunity to reproduce and take up residence in someone else. Thoughts go through a Darwinian process that favors the ones with staying power and transmissibility. Thoughts that revolve around survival issues stay with us from generation-to-generation. Many thoughts form around a composite of issues, such as security, finding a mate, and providing for a family. The useful thoughts in this vein are concerned with directing the will to the benefit of the organism and its progeny. They involve planning productive activities and reacting to situations as they arise. These thoughts are not problematic when they are applied to issues that they are capable of resolving. But such a thought that has been given enough energy can go rogue. Prudence can give way to paranoia if one focuses too much energy on what could go wrong.

You should be getting the idea that thoughts are travelers that take up residence in the mind. Some of them are useful and serve a function. Some are merely benign, such as trivial thoughts, and others are malignant and deeply negative. They serve no purpose but to steal energy and self perpetuate. Thoughts do spread from person-to-person, teacher to student, parent to child, etc. In this way a thought lives for many generations, "crowdsurfing" through minds. Social media has created a whole new channel through which thoughts can connect with host minds.

The mind's fundamental strategy is not dependent on your constant misery. In fact, the mind is probably most secure in those for whom things are going well. My effort to subordinate the mind to the consciousness stemmed from a disappointment that I could not accept. My mind became like a "frenemy" who was constantly reminding me how I'd never have what I really wanted. It had done this before, and each time I'd adjust my life to silence it. But this time, there was no way to get around the obstacle. I was not going to get what I wanted. I could not tolerate the thought of being deprived of what I thought I needed to be whole, and so I sought a way to silence the thinking. The pain must be severe and persistent enough to motivate your escape.

CHAPTER FIFTEEN
Quieting the Mind

A child finds joy more easily than an adult because they are less "filled" with thoughts and have more stillness of consciousness. As the mind takes up more space, it crowds out pure consciousness. The mind is threatened by consciousness because both require a certain resource, "space." Being occupied by pure consciousness precludes domination by the mind and vice versa. Distillation of consciousness from thought is our natural path to joy, and it is not dependent on any outside circumstance. This peace of consciousness occupies you when you have absolutely no cares in the world. Like the moment your ticket shows the winning lottery numbers. Stillness of consciousness expands from your innermost being. It is completely free to those who surrender into inner-silence and inner-stillness, and accessing it requires that you merely make room for it and dwell therein as awareness. You make room for consciousness by emptying your head of thoughts. When thoughts are absent, the mind can get no traction on the emotions. The state of pure consciousness is joy of the permanent kind. It's always there, you just need to be still and quiet within. Pure consciousness is the joy that cures the crave for which the mind is prescribing more outside things. When you've discovered how to quiet your mind and have it reacting to concrete-stimuli-only, you will again find the place of pure consciousness, but now with the powerful tool of a well-governed mind at your command.

When the mind is quiet, the being engages sometimes less than what can be apprehended by the five senses, but they are free of thought, which stills consciousness, and from this stillness emerges another sense, the one that palpably feels the perpetual joy and peace that is now known to be endogenous, of no outside origin, dependent on no outside thing. The owner of a quiet mind accepts the pace at which life comes and deals with issues as they present themselves and only when they present themselves. Planning that's done beforehand is addressed in its own time. This doesn't preclude being generally prepared for what may come unexpectedly, but the constant running through of scenarios in your mind will rob you of happiness. Don't think about tomorrow or yesterday. Rich is the man who in simple surroundings, can think "I want to hang on to right now." That's how good it should feel just going about your business. All the sweeter when happy things come.

Be cautious about where and when you take your mind. Recall the emotional minefield of interconnected thoughts, and ask yourself where such minefields exist. They live in your conception of the past. Your mind thinks the past is a safe place because it knows what happened there, but it is just the devil you know. The past is a sad place, full of nostalgia and longing, as well as regrets. Everything could just explode into emotions if you want to dance with those ghosts. Keep your head out of the past. It is a prison.

Your conception of the future has some pleasant thoughts, but also many anxieties. Daydreams are the junk food of your consciousness and will spoil your appetite for reality, leading one to seek elevation through addictive substitutes. I've come to believe that daydreaming is the siren song of addiction. When reality never lives up to the daydreams, we search for worldly ways to sate the appetite that has been whetted. Don't daydream too much or worry either. The universe isn't malformed. We are like the universe in that we create, but we are in fact, a part of the universe itself. We are instruments of the universe, part of its creative faculties. We are the bristles of the artist's brush, and you are shaping the finer details of the piece. Do not worry about the nature of the stroke that you make on the canvas. Have faith in the artist.

Whereas the past and future live only in your mind, the present is real. Everything is much closer to what it seems in the present. You don't have to worry about paying emotional interest, anxiety for the future and regret for the past. You will be happier if you deal with emotions in the present, as they arise. You don't struggle with or resist them. You just let them happen inside you without trying to force anything. You just play dead for that Grizzly Bear, and let it slip away. It is important enough to reiterate that you need to deal with your emotions as they arise, but don't act out on them, unless needed. Feel them, and don't resist how they make you feel. This will keep the amount of emotional energy that is "on tap" at a minimum. Less pent up emotion means that negative thoughts are less likely to awaken. This is very important. A body full of pent up emotion will not have a quiet mind.

One key to reigning-in unwanted thoughts is to gradually shorten the span of time from which you draw them. Reducing the real-estate available to thoughts will also reduce their population. Pick a time in the recent past and future and set them as boundaries for a "time blinder" beyond which you don't let your mind wander. You could wake up one morning and decide that work-planning aside, you're going to think only of things that are going on right now. Just as blinders on a horse narrow its field of vision, installing time blinders on your mind will narrow the scope of time from which you draw thoughts. The narrower the timeframe you can achieve, the fewer thoughts you will have and the less likely they will be to have an emotional charge.

Another way to conceptualize the mind that may help you quiet it is to consider its complexity relative to that of an animal. The animal brain can't entertain thoughts of the past and future; it has to live in the present. If brains were engines, the animal brain would be a three-cylinder, and yours would be a V8. It's not possible to make your V8 as fuel-efficient as the smaller engine, but there is a feature which helps bring the V8 into more efficient territory. It's called "variable displacement," and it allows the engine to shut off half of the cylinders when the power isn't needed. You'll never make your brain as consistently quiet as that of an animal, but you can shut down some cylinders when not called for. In particular, you want to shut down the memory cylinder and the daydreaming cylinder.

CHAPTER SIXTEEN
Temporal Harmonizing

Since all things being equal, a pleasant reality is preferred to a fantasy of it, the mind needs to create content that eclipses the day-to-day life of the individual. For example, if you had a choice between eating your favorite food and just thinking about it, you would have the real version. To distract from the moment, the mind has to create fantastical visions of wonderful things to which a normal reality cannot compare. It may also create fears to which you must pay attention. While it's difficult to think of nothing, it is relatively easy to intentionally think of something specific. This fact can be used to help quiet the mind by pulling the creative faculty of attention away from it.

As you let go of the mind's noise, it might be chattering away about any number of things. The mind is a movement that identifies as a self, and so it fears stillness as death. It would resist the moment rather than surrender to silence. Some people have trouble keeping their mouth shut, but quieting the mind is even harder. To temporally harmonize, pick an object in your field of view, preferably something small with defined borders that fall entirely within your field of vision. A candle in the dark is ideal. Close your eyes, letting that object be the last thing you see, and mentally visualize it. Now open your eyes and stare at it again while trying to keep the mental image of it in mind. Repeat the process several times, looking at it, closing your eyes, visualizing it, and then opening them. Each time the mental image fades, you may feel a "focusing" of the real image. This should start to pull your mind away from wherever it was and bring it into reality.

Intentionally imagining something will pull your mind away from wherever it was and into what you're trying to picture, which happens to be an object in your immediate field of vision. And by depriving the sense through which you've captured the thing you're imagining, it allows you to more easily visualize the object. This creates a stronger pull on the mind, bringing it into an imagined space that looks just like reality. However, when you open your eyes, the reality will supersede the imagined counterpart, for two reasons, first is that it's hard to picture something in your head while you're looking right at it. Second, the signal coming in from reality is so much stronger and more vibrant than the copycat image your mind can produce, which causes the mind to "harmonize" with reality. When given the choice between two identical images, one from reality, the other created by the mind's imagination, the consciousness will tune in on the real one.

As you meditate, you're doing it with the aim of quieting thoughts by letting them pass, leaving only the sensation of being an observer. When thoughts interrupt, repeat the temporal harmonizing to pull you away from them. When all is quiet, you will feel space inside you. If you focus on your body in this state, you may be able to feel waves of energy flowing through you. It is a warm and pleasant energy.

Another way to quiet the mind is by seizing the imaginary "I." The voice that chatters in your head can be difficult to silence, like you're trying to stop up a dam that keeps springing more leaks. The thoughts that seem to arise spontaneously can be overpowered by a pre-selected thought. It's possible to use the "inner microphone" to impose a silence on the mind. Seizing the imaginary "I" involves taking over the voice in your mind and just saying "I..." with a long pause, as if you were going to say something but had a long stutter or had forgotten the words. This creates a gap in the thinking, and you can keep increasing this gap of silence. While doing this, feel the place from which this "I" thought arises. It comes from the spiritual heart, where you feel emotions in playing dead for the Grizzly. Hold the concept of this "I" to that place and do not let it link itself up with other concepts. Pull the "I" into the spiritual heart and feel it dissolve. The "I" is a thought, an observable thing, and as such, it is not you, for it has a witness. With the "I" thought withering in the spiritual heart, its witness will be liberated in silence. The deliberate use of words facilitates the control of the gaps in between. Keep doing it, and this "filibustering" the mind with silence will reveal the changeless before which all changeful things pass. Similar practices have been used for thousands of years in the east.

Once pure consciousness has cut out a beachhead of stillness in the inner-space, it becomes easier to quiet the mind. If pure consciousness is continuously occupying more internal space, it leaves less room for the movement of mind. A mind that occupies less space cannot speak so loudly or persistently, especially if you've been keeping residual emotional energy in check. The chattering and uncontrollable part of the mind starts to recede.

The laying-dormant of the uncontrolled mind short-circuits the compulsions that characterize obsession and process-addiction. It also prevents boredom in mundane circumstances. The cravings are lost without losing the ability to enjoy the activities formerly-craved. It stops obsessions because the part of the mind that digs them up like some overzealous dog is itself, lying dormant. It's like you're engaging only the useful parts of your mind. You've reshaped the neural pathways to bypass the places where all the garbage is stored, and for lack of engagement, the garbage decays into stillness. A person is just the reflection of impressions in consciousness that, in their totality, are believed to be a self by their witness. When the belief that anything is less than perfect is dropped, the surrender to this perfection resolves these impressions, and in the resultant stillness of consciousness, the illusion of a changeful self is dispelled.

CHAPTER SEVENTEEN
The Realm of Consciousness

When something brings you intense happiness, is it not like there is nothing so sublime as to be with the object of your affection? Everything draws down to the moment. You are temporarily "untethered" from the weight of the past and worry of the future. It's the feeling we get when something is so appealing that it captures our focus and allows us to drop our accumulated cares. This feeling is the light of pure consciousness shining in. Pure consciousness is the raw spark that filled you when the universe formed you from itself. The part of you that was awake before you learned to put words to things. It is pure, having neither judgement, nor positionality. It is the universe observing itself through you, and it has a sense of wonder about everything, and when you were a child, it was unobstructed by thoughts.

The real "You" can no more exist in the realm of imagination than an imaginary thing can exist in reality. Reality is not of the past or the future; it is of right now. This is because the seer, consciousness, can experience something only as it happens. All else is a recollection of the past or projection of the future. What is it that recounts or projects? It is the mind talking to consciousness. Consciousness cannot fully experience reality when the mind is feeding it a recollection or projection from the imagination. All that is "not now" exists in the mind-only. The only way for consciousness to fully emerge from the waters of imagination and into reality is for it to no longer be subject to the recollections and projections of the mind.

When you have continually felt and surrendered to negative emotions as they've arisen, and quieted your mind and limited it to performing tasks that relate to immediate needs, you have entered the realm of consciousness. The inner-voice is mute, and it's like something that has been obstructing your view is gone. The lack of unbridled thoughts and negative emotions inside you will have created space into which consciousness will naturally flow. You should begin to feel much more positive and contented. Your cravings and desires should naturally blunt themselves. You will still be able to enjoy the good things in life, but you will not feel the insatiable desire for them. There will be fewer cravings. Just as you will be dealing with pain only as it arises, you will feel the enjoyment of a thing only as it arises. Separating your higher-self from your mind gives you a different internal vantage point. Instead of being "close" to your thoughts, you hear them coming. You begin to feel apart from your thoughts. Internal quiet makes a rising thought more noticeable, like a noisy person who has just walked into the library. Escort the thought out of your mind by harmonizing with reality. You can walk away from a thought. As consciousness expands in you, it will be felt as an energy. It will feel like a mix of all good emotions, but it will not be of emotional origin, for it will not correlate with thoughts but rather a lack of them. It is a perpetual state of living as a joyful energy that can expand beyond the body in which it dwells.

Whereas there's a great benefit to dealing with pain only as it arises, there are also benefits to feeling the enjoyment only as it arises, and this is the key to overcoming addictions centered on the bodily appetites. When you feel enjoyment only as it arises, you are not anticipating it. Anticipation is on the path to craving, and craving is on the road to addiction. Having a quiet mind, well-governed emotions, and a focus on reality, has the effect of moderating the appetites. As alluded to in earlier chapters, the level of excitement you need to become aroused is a function of your normal intake of stimulation. Addictions to sex, games, and food are all based on a need to elevate the consciousness. Doing these things makes the addict feel alive while they're doing them. However, if your baseline of stimulation is lower because you've trained yourself to deal with reality only as it arises, you get a greater elevation of consciousness relative to external stimulation. You won't need a reality that's close to your wildest fantasies to feel fulfilled, and on top of that, the fulfillment will be longer-lasting.

Consciousness is who you are in the absence of thought, your spirit. Your mind at the infant stage was not capable of thinking in words, and there were no memories on which to draw and indeed no concept of time. And yet, you perceived. As you grew and developed, your mind figured out how to use words and name objects and learn their use. But before the myriad of thoughts came in and your mind started building them into something that would identify as you, there was you. Some people have the ability to recall memories from early childhood. These memories help us know that there was a time when we were pure consciousness. Pure consciousness is the contentment of the infant when all of its needs are being met. Unlike the body, consciousness has no outside needs. The body needs to be alive in order to be the receiver of consciousness, but consciousness does not need a particular body to arise.

Consciousness is eternal; creating windows for its self-observation is the purpose of the universe. Even when life on Earth ends, there will be consciousness. In the lifetime of the universe, the amount of time it took for our world to go from a hot rock to having humans is but the blink of an eye. Just as the internet doesn't disappear when your computer breaks, the potential for consciousness to emerge from the universe doesn't cease when a particular body/species/world ends. Your body is a construct that arose from the universe to be filled with consciousness that also arose from the universe. You are a mechanism through which the universe observes itself. You are a manifestation of the universe's consciousness, and when you die, that consciousness will recede back to the place from whence it came. It's not necessary to grasp how it really happens to appreciate the truth of it.

All consciousness needs is to be allowed. Consciousness is the end, whereas the mind and body are means, intended to be facilitators of life in this world. Mind and body are the "space suit" that allows consciousness to access the material world. They are a necessary burden. Consciousness is the only thing of which you cannot have too much; imbalance between it and the other two elements is always a function of the latter's proportions, as consciousness expands and contracts relative to the others. The other realms exist as facilitators only. The emotions are the power plant, and the mind is the bureaucracy. The Consciousness is you. The default state of consciousness is joy. When its emotions are not being activated by external needs, a baby is happy and finds wonder in all things. Consciousness requires that there be internal space in you for it to occupy. In most people, consciousness is crowded out by thoughts. Your level of consciousness is a function of the amount of space you've left for it, net of your thoughts. Your level of consciousness is automatically optimized when your mind is governed by boundaries that limit its scope of duties to the practical, e.g., driving, working, solving problems as they arise, etc. Allow your mind to do its job, but don't let it occupy all of your inner space.

A Note on Relationships and "The One"

Regret from a failed relationship is a source of pain that whispers in your ear "you could have had it all." It's telling you that "it" was the path to happiness, and that you missed it. You blew it. There's no way back, and as a consequence, you'll never be happy. You missed the one. That is not true. People seem to cross our path for a reason. A "soulmate" might not be someone you were meant to be with. Sometimes being star-crossed causes such pain that it precipitates a spiritual awakening. Regarding relationships in-general, if you are unhappy while unattached, there's almost no way that you can have a successful relationship. The reason for this is that a partner will indeed elevate your consciousness for a time, taking away all of your cares and bringing you joy...again, for a time. However, our mind/ego, will eventually become habituated to that person, and then all the troubles we perceived prior to the relationship will seep back into our minds, and we'll be unhappy again; only this time we may blame the other person for it.

The best way to be successful in relationships is to first be happy with yourself. You must find the internal way to manage your cares, one that doesn't involve an outside lever to temporarily push them aside. This is done by continuously living in the moment, perceiving the world as it is, without letting any thoughts or media color or distort it. True and lasting happiness is not a function of anything outside of yourself, not even "the one," for nothing endures. Everything will eventually leave you or die, and so if you're staking your happiness on any outside thing, you're going to be left with dust and memories, which are bittersweet at best. No, the true joy comes from the unobstructing of what always shines underneath, pure consciousness. Help your loved one cultivate pure consciousness in themselves, and you will both have "the one."

CHAPTER EIGHTEEN
Going Forward

My hope is that the preceding chapters frame the inner-problem in a way that helps the reader get a toehold on whatever obsessions and/or process-addictions he/she may have. I have found that living according to this paradigm and conducting my life in a way that is mindful of its system of consequences has helped me overcome obsessions and process-addictions, as well as put me in a state where I'm not likely to fall back into them. This way of thinking is not new. It has been written about for thousands of years in the teachings of Taoism, Hinduism, Buddhism, and to a less acknowledged extent, Christianity. There are very likely more. These practices can also help you get over recent and past hurts. These are tools that you can use every day and know when, how, and why to apply them.

Charity is not just in what you give, it's in how you treat other people and live your life. When one has subordinated the mind to consciousness, then it is impossible to be anything but charitable. You may find that you feel more interconnected with people, even strangers. If you have ever entertained a racist thought, it would be much harder with a mind that has quit blaming others. You realize that the "other" arose in and from the same universe as you. Another reason for this feeling of universality is that when you have stripped away the noise, all that is left is the observing part of you, and it has a consistency to it that one could not imagine varying from person-to-person. People who are filled with consciousness are in alignment with each other in that there is no positionality in the absence of thought.

I highly recommend you be selective about sourcing your news. I heard of a woman who lived to be almost 102, and she said that she never watches the news. I know this is merely anecdotal, but I do believe that much of the mass media has a negative slant, but we're collectively responsible. The media makes a living at arbitraging eyeballs. Whatever stories attract the most will be the ones that fill the headlines. In this way, the very news that's reported is a reflection of our appetite for either positivity or negativity; supply meets demand. There will always be both good and bad news, but the proportion of each that's reported in the mass media is more a function of the readers than the editors. The editors' motivation is economic, a constant, but the appetite of the reader is the variable, and it varies directly with the level of consciousness.

CHAPTER NINETEEN
In Summary

Stay aware of your negative thoughts and emotions, and manage them through surrender right when they arise. Try to quiet your mind, and especially don't let it go wandering into the past and the future. Use the practicess to draw your focus into reality. Try focusing on an object in your field of view. Remember how it looks and close your eyes and visualize it. Now open them and repeat the process. Create gaps in-between the words in your mind and try to make them expand. Generally try to keep your "inner mouth" closed. Don't let it prattle on like a drunk. Try to do this perpetually. When you've made these practices a part of your daily life, you should begin to experience a change. You should feel less-burdened and generally more satisfied. You should also feel a cessation of the bodily drives, as well as an absence of thoughts that have been consuming you. You will feel "distance" between you and your thoughts. You will be more able to hold them at arm's-length and know that they are phantoms, and therefore, don't need to be granted emotional energy. They will wither away. You will also find that you experience more joy from the little things in life. You will not be easily drawn into pathological or self-destructive habits, nor arguments. Instead of "seeking" things, you will be satisfied to see everything come to you in its own time.

In Conclusion

It is logical to expect a reduction in stress when a decrease in thinking puts one in contact with fewer emotionally-charged thoughts and memories. The reduction in thought also relieves obsessions in that they are thought-based. No thoughts means no obsessions. To the extent that thoughts play a role as mental triggers in addictive behaviors, their disappearance helps break the cycle. These practices can help you govern the mind, and because the brain is malleable, you will see results if you keep trying. It will get easier to create silence as your brain creates new neural pathways. Eventually you will feel that something akin to an "off switch" has formed in your brain. You will catch yourself thinking idle thoughts, and be able to turn them off like a light that you almost left on when leaving a room. Let silence be your refuge.

CHAPTER TWENTY
Meditations

Meditations

The following section is provided as a supplement to the practices given in the book. They are short writings on the nature of consciousness that arise spontaneously from the meditative state. Reading these will support you in your journey to Self.

***

To believe that the predominant mental state lays legitimate claim to sanity, simply by virtue of its majority status, is an error. If one carefully examines what constitutes a normal state of mind, it can be seen that it does not actually operate according to reality, but rather, the realm of imaginary things, taking its cues not from the moment, but rather, from how the store of mental debris reacts to it. This, in absolute terms, is to be separated from reality by a layer of unreality, which is insanity. To be in Truth is to abandon the imaginary and operate solely as the pure consciousness that witnessed the events from which the now-surrendered conditioning was constructed. The mind fears this kind of purity, believing it to be a pathological state, but whereas the psychopath has desire without attachment, the saint has neither, for in emptiness of mind there is revealed the fullness of heart, and thus, no void to fill.

***

What persists in humans is the propensity to be programmed and the inability to see that programming as what the Self sees and not the Self itself. Conflict is the defense of form and programming. The programming that's established is arbitrarily determined by position in time and space, as well as the events upstream of birth that provide the sensing body and its tendencies. This is karma. There is no peace to be found in these changeful phenomena, but their witness is the hidden peace that's ever-sought in the futility of stabilizing the changeful, itself being completely stable and without qualities. The seeking of this peace on the part of itself is what hides it. Realizing peace is a matter of letting go of all that changes through the recognition and acceptance of its changeful nature.

***

True Love

False love is as the light that shines through identically-positioned holes in two stacked pieces of paper. The paper is the imaginary fabric of identity, and the holes are the things held in common, e.g., family, race, culture, and every other imagined overlapping affiliation that removes threat. For the one who identifies with the superficial, there is no love shining through when the holes don't overlap with the "other" whom they behold. With true love there is no paper person to hide the light, for it has been burned up in the fire of the heart.

***

There's something about surrendering to the reality of not getting what you want, particularly if your desire is both great and greatly-frustrated. If you surrender deeply enough, and truly feel it in your heart, and then hand it over to a higher power, it will take the associated thoughts with it. This "stripping" of vagrant thoughts, through surrender, can reveal that the true source of happiness is within, and that you are that Happiness itself, for what good thing in life isn't known by how it makes you feel? The fire is an expression of its fuel. What's felt is your deepest essence, which is not a thought. This frustrated life can be a blessing in that it provides impetus to excavate the negative energies that underlie the thoughts that hide who we truly are, which is their witness.

***

Some alkali metals will combust upon contact with atmospheric moisture. And so is it with the peace of the spiritual heart when exposed to the light of reality. When buried in the vibration of thoughts, be they good or bad, It is not perceptible, but when there stands no thought between the moment and its witness, an irreversible explosion of peace can result. This is far less likely to happen when the dross of the mind is sweet like sugar, when life is good and the thoughts are palatable. The dream is sweet enough to sustain sleep. But when there is a huge gap between "what is" and what's held in mind as the ideal, the frustration will either bring a doubling-down on action to manifest the desire, which is eternal frustration, or surrender to the reality of its absence. In the latter case, the true and ever-present Self may be realized when the resulting gap between the thought and its Seer, exposes the mind as being a false identity. This is to forever know yourself as the unchanging peace that hides behind every eye. Its apparent departure or absence is merely the belief in illusion. Its unchanging perfection reveals unity with the Absolute.

***

The believer is a thinker
The non-believer is a thinker
The Knower is not a thinker but a feeler,
for what is thought is what is felt,
and what can be thought is not real but imaginary, and what's felt in the noise of the imaginary is the unconscious desire for the Real, which is suffering. But by feeling what cannot be thought, desire is killed. In silence the heart discovers itself by feel, and thinking is then abandoned for knowing, and suffering is traded for peace. Who is the Knower but the Knowing?
***

The joy of the moment is in its truth, not its content. When you dream in sleep, the point of perception is a single "dot" that views the dream as an external world. You may notice that when you awake, you would typically like to go back to sleep and dream some more, regardless of how mundane the dream's content. The apprehension of this one-pointed "dot mind" is the source of the joy in the dream, not the content. This mode of perception is devoid of the inner-editorial that normally dilutes the joy of the one-pointed "dreamer's mind." In the normal waking state, the point of perception grows from a dot to a foggy circle, the fog being thoughts, the mind, the ego, conditioning; they are all descriptions of the same thing.

The foggy circle is a mental construct built from your programming, e.g., media, education, culture, upbringing, and experiences. It's the false self, not your friend! In the foggy circle, the fog is a volatile medium that feels vulnerable and fearful of all countervailing positions, i.e., other egos. It is a torture chamber that traps the dot, but very few see this. The fog separates the dot from reality, hence the term "unconsciousness."

Most see the foggy circle as the dot itself; they think it's the true Self. The being who has achieved liberation has realized their position as the dot while still in the waking state.   They have shrunken the foggy circle to the point where is has sunken back into the dot, which is found on the right side of the chest, next to the physical heart. This is actually what happens temporarily when you are doing something fun or pleasurable. You are wholly in the moment, and the fog of thought has for a time, sunken back into the dot. This is why you can feel bliss in your chest when you get your heart's desire. You have no thoughts or cares for a time. This inner-arrangement is the unseen source of joy, not the novel content that induces it. That outer thing need not even change for it to lose its ability to stem the mental tide. This is why we become jaded and then run to the next thing.

The most direct spiritual teacher says "just keep quiet."   The teacher wants you to realize "the dot" through inner-silence, to be the true Self, the dot that knows the world as an extension of itself.   However, few are ripe for this realization. Instead, they must go through the dark night of the soul that reveals the ego and sees the death of all but its "utility thoughts." The excavation process is to surrender this ego by feeling its emotional products wholly, without resistance, and surrendering them to a higher power as they present themselves.   Then the person must keep the ego from coming back by learning to stay present. You can do this by corralling all thoughts to the right side of your chest within the noose of a single thought that can be discarded when no longer needed. That thought is "I AM." Perpetually think "I AM" as you inhale, then have no thoughts on the top, no thoughts on the exhale, and no thoughts on the bottom, repeat, repeat, repeat...

***

Learning to swim involves going into the water without a floatation device. Similarly, spiritual practice is contented living without the aid of props to pull one's attention out of the chaotic mind. A person with no spiritual practice, when stripped of their material comforts, will suffer an existential crisis; like a non-swimmer thrown into the water without a float, they will flounder. But in this drowning process of loss, a fortunate soul may be saved by surrender. This is accepting that the universe unfolds perfectly as is, and that our ego-inspired plots and schemes are not necessarily in harmony with it. These willful second-guesses are like the flails of a drowning man; they aim to preserve life, and entail great effort but are totally ineffective. The adept swimmer can float in the water with almost no effort just by staying calm. Surrender, holding no resistance to the moment, regardless of what the panicking mind wants to do.

***

The Spiritual Paradigm
There are many ways to communicate what follows. These words are truly irrelevant and can be discarded upon the discovery of that to which they

point. They can be taken as a mere map that describes particular landmarks with certain words. Others have written such maps and describe different landmarks that point to the same discovery. They are just metaphors denominated in the currency of words, which must be thrown away.

Everything is formed through a spiritual medium that man has given many names, e.g., Spirit, Consciousness, Shakti, etc. In the Holy Bible, where God says "let there be light," the word of God gave form to this medium, and what we see in this very moment continues to be held together by His will, the product of which could be called the mind of God. Others point not to a personified God but to a causal chain from which consciousness arises. We personally cannot know, for nothing in a dream can know the dreamer, but who witnesses the dream? To us, the unfolding of man's world seems unreasonably chaotic and unfair, but the scriptures describe it as being exactly so, turbulent, a sea of change in which security is an illusion pursued by those blinded by it.

Religion is as a blind man's description, passed to him from another who saw. Such glimpses are misinterpreted or distorted over time by those who lack the first-hand knowledge, for having been only able to frame them in terms of the gross. Such would be the Pharisee, the inquisitor, the prosperity preacher, and all those who do not teach us to look within ourselves to find the Kingdom. But look inside we must, before we can know the magnificence of creation for what it is, before we can perceive the sense in which our own being is in the likeness of its creator. If we remain on the surface of it, in ignorance, it's because our attachment to its superficial aspect causes fear that puts us into a resistance of now that veils its Truth.

To go beyond belief and conjecture, we must come out of resistance and surrender wholly to God's will, which is the unfolding of what's before you in this very moment. There are five aspects to a human that are revealed in the unfolding of Self-knowledge:

- **The physical form or gross body** - Everyone knows this form and many believe it to be the totality of what we are. When people speak of what's beyond this, some will say it's "make believe" and blind faith. But for those who have sufficiently explored with their God-given faculties, who have earnestly inquired into their own nature, it has given them an experiential knowledge of these hidden things. Though faith allowed them to investigate this, the discovery moves them out of faith and into knowledge.

- **The intellect** - this faculty of intellect is a product of the physical body and the energy that moves it. Intellect gives the power of discrimination, the ability to measure and weigh things based upon what the senses convey to it. Were the being a computer, this would be the CPU.

- **The mind** - the mind has two aspects, that which is actively manifested by the power of attention, which is the sum of thoughts being observed, i.e., the conscious mind, and that which lies dormant as the sum of impressions born of experience. The active is the ego in motion, and the inactive is the store of karma. The former arises from the latter as attention is given to parts of it. Again, were we a computer, these two would be the data held in RAM and ROM, respectively.

- **The energetic or subtle body** - The three aforementioned bodies are movements within this aspect, arising from it. How we feel is a product of how we have "colored" this energy with our thoughts, actions, and what we take into ourselves, i.e., food and substances. Gross matter, emotions, and thoughts are woven of this fabric in "thread-counts" descending from gross to subtle. In surrender to God's will, the emotions and thoughts relax to a more subtle state of this energy. In repose, it is physically felt and reveals itself to be the true currency of gratification, felt temporarily in the sating of desires. It is tasted when there is excitement, but it departs upon the loss of novelty. In other words, experiences do nothing but make us feel a certain way within ourselves. When "what is" and what's desired come into alignment by virtue of circumstance, the tensions that give form to thought and emotion fall away, causing them to revert to their natural state, which is peace. This is to move closer to the likeness in which God made us. In resistance, thoughts and emotions tighten and form a wall that hides peace, and the drive to come out of this tension is called desire, which is the suffering that increases as we move away from God. As you move towards your true nature, which is peace, you get closer to God, for God made you in His likeness. Hell is nothing more than separation from God through resistance to the unfolding of His creation. This is why the atheist and existentialist cannot perceive beyond the gross. In their belief in only the temporary, the gross, their fear creates a tension that walls them off from feeling the peace of their true nature.

- **The spiritual heart** - This is the mustard seed to which Jesus referred in the Holy Bible. This is the door on which Christ knocks in Revelation. The error that Christians make is not in believing that Christ can come into their hearts and set them free, but rather, in taking for granted that they are already in touch with the heart from which we are born again in His likeness. In lacking the faith to surrender to this moment, by hiding in thought, they dwell in the mind and thus, their God is an imaginary idol born of resistance, a genie who would grant them more of the things they seek in their fear-inspired quest to preserve the changeful. Everything that cultivates thoughts is building this resistance, this attachment to the temporary. In dropping all of this, the mind becomes the still water of the spiritual heart. In this stillness, we direct our attention to it, and it's as if God looks over our shoulder and directs the creative power of His attention to both grow the spiritual heart and give us the reward of His Love through its reflection. The mustard seed grows into a soul that bears the likeness of its witness, which cannot be described but only pointed to.

The path that Christ showed man is that of surrender, as He certainly had the agency to resist the Father's will, but in not doing so, He was and is one with the Father. We are the same stuff of which He is, but it is incumbent upon us to transmute it into its natural state. The resolution of the ego is the path. It is the dropping of thoughts through a persistent focus on God and His creation, which is this very moment. If you were to do nothing but perpetually agree with what is by replacing all thought with an "amen," while surrendering to the feelings of emotions and giving them over to God, there would be a discovery. The impetus to dedicate oneself to this is called grace. Every true spiritual practice works towards this union with God through surrender, by dying to oneself. Another way would be to simply inquire over and over, "who am I?" In this question, which precludes other thoughts, God's answer regarding your true nature will come, not in words, but in silence.

The purity of a spiritual practice is known by the end towards which it works. Spiritual practices that are in alignment with worldly goals are nothing more than black magic that takes one further from God and the punishment of separation in illusion.

***

When the protagonist acts to bring light, it casts a shadow upon those who do not appear within the

93

hero's perspective. It is from behind the walls of identity that might makes right, but it's only right for some and never all. For who doesn't believe that they are the good guy? The identity is a concept, and concepts are the blanket that hides who we really are. The other whom you wish to fix wants equally to fix you. The form is arbitrary, as is the conditioning, and as such, one variety has no merit over the other, for it's the wall of thought that falls between these subsets that brings out identical vices in each, when given power. When you die unto yourself, you can kill the other in like fashion, but so long as the person lives within you, you will see others because of your blindness.

    ***

The person, as in the mind, is a movement on the face of the heart, but in surrendering to the divine will, which is what is, it resolves into stillness and reflects the countenance of its witness.

    ***

Identity is ignorance of Self.

Identity is ignorance of God.

Identity is the mote in thy brother's eye and the beam in thine own.

From Identity arises hate, oppression, murder, and war.

The cultivator of identity damns you with the sweet poison of being special.

You are not the identity.

To know this is to discover everlasting peace.

Find the root of identity, which is the thought that says "I."

Surrender to all that it resists, all that it fears.

Find the heart from which it arises, and hold this "I" perpetually to the flames of it.

In silence, the "I" dissolves into the heart and reveals in it, the reflection of Who you really are, beyond the fabric of imagination from which identity is woven.

To live as the imagined person is to live in fear for it and die with it. You are not your body or mind, but the Love who witnesses the heart that reflects it. Discover It and know true Love.

***

Identity is the sum of differences between what is and what's desired. It's temporary, has fear, and thinks it's owed something, e.g., peace, love, wealth, fame, justice, eternal life, etc., but in reality, this construct of wants, of thoughts, stunts the unfolding of the soul because it perpetually holds attention apart from the moment, which is the very unfolding of creation. It hides what it seeks. For the love-of and fear-for the temporary, we miss the eternal. So cling to your identity, your race, politics, religion, etc., these hemmed-in things that will forever be at war with a counterpoint. Hide from the moment in them, and when you've suffered enough at the prospect of their inevitable thwarting and destruction, turn your attention away from the mind and surrender the feeling of its resistances to the heart. Stay in the moment. There you will see that you are the eternal witness of these changeful things, and as such, are unchanging, just as the Love that hides behind every other body and perspective. If it changes, it's not you, for you were made in the image of the unchanging.

***

95

You will never bring the other into alignment with your position if it's mutually-exclusive to theirs. This will remain so as long as there are those we call others. What if we found the building blocks of "other" within ourselves, saw them dispassionately, and acknowledged them as arbitrarily given and not necessarily constituting some merit? Who isn't proud of their particulars, even if that pride stems from having rejected a bit of one's perceived lot? Identity is the mote in our own eye, not because of its content, but because of its status as illusion and not this very place of unfolding. It is infidelity to Now that divides us. Identity can live in nowhere but time, imagination. We chase echoes and so the noise that hides the One Love never stops. They are thoughts, and by seeing their circumstantial nature, we can see how they are merely phenomena that can be viewed without judgement. Consciousness will react to the stimuli in the same manner given the identical vibration. You are the consciousness that reacted to entry through this window of time/space, and "he," the other, is the same consciousness reacting to different circumstances. We are like raindrops where some hit the dirt and some hit the river, and some hit the ocean. Dispelling the illusion that one is anything but the water is the way to discovery. The world can only come together when people surrender who they think they are in order to discover the One who saw the concept of itself arise. The freshness of presence affords no accumulation of dissatisfaction, which is the stuff of which an identity is made. Do we get more or less fun when we take ourselves seriously?

    ***

Behavior is a function of form and conditioning. Form is unchanging in the aggregate. How behavior changes from one generation to the next is a function of conditioning. What two generations hold in common is the propensity to identify with form and conditioning. The variable is environmental. Whoever controls the flow of information controls the behavior of a generation. Human problems arise from both programming and the unconsciousness required to be moved by it.

Some will conform to whatever life the screens prescribe; others will rebel, partially or wholly. Surface strategies for this involve insulating one's own from the stream of programming, building a more wholesome person through traditions. But even traditions are eroded by exposure of the impressionable young to the programmed culture.

The variable of conditioning is not true and timeless; meaning, the same form will yield a different expression when exposed to different environments. Thus, the authentic Self is not any version of conditioning. In surrendering to the pain of what one believes to be their own thoughts, there comes the recognition that their (thoughts) ability to hurt comes from the loyalty we give them. In unconsciousness this loyalty is automatic, in awakening, as impossible as unseeing what was seen.

The recognition of one's automatic acceptance of the arbitrary is what breaks the legitimacy of conditioning's claim to loyalty. What if we saw what the world has made us think we are and let go of it?

Who are we really? Ask this to the exclusion of all thoughts.

Love, freedom, peace, joy, bliss, are all expressions of the essential nature of consciousness. Everything is consciousness, but in the absence of movement, the medium of consciousness is unbound love. We think we come into this freedom, but it is us, and what we took to be us is just a movement within us. We've always been free, but in realizing it, that freedom sees how what it took itself to be was just an echo of its own unfolding.

The walls of the invisible prison have a voice. Freedom is seeing the arbitrary nature of that voice and letting it slip out of awareness through surrender to and thus unity with Now.

The phantoms of the schizophrenic have merely jumped to the other side of perception. The average person encounters the same cast of characters within the mind. They are often allowed to speak without being questioned, since their presence is quite normal. The heeded inner voice, not the knowing of quietude, but the one who blames, belittles, makes excuses, covets, envies, is wrathful, lustful, obstinate, and greedy, that voice is the author of suffering, and its muse is the fear of Now. It wants to be anywhere but here and now, and fittingly, it is no more real than the imaginary G Men from "A Beautiful Mind." The moment dissolves such things.

The voice fears change because it is subject to change. It wants to deny change and preserve the illusion of its persistence. It is wax that fears melting, not knowing that all it will lose is its shape. So long as it frets over this, it cannot apprehended its waxness.

If it surrenders to the moment, it will drop the tent poles of experience that prop up its provincial form. Surrender unshackles consciousness from the fetters of what's feared or desired. In this absence of definition, the end that believed itself to be the means stops chasing its tail and rests in the reward of its Self.

***

Truth is not what's in your mind, memory or any history book. These things hide Truth behind their fearful, longing, vengeful, and hopeful vibrations. Truth is a door that's in front of you 24/7. It is the moment, obscured by the thoughts we take to be ourselves. Truth is the you who stares back at you from behind the eyes of every "other."

The ego is retained content bound by emotional energy. It's a ball of words and energy, the flavor of which depends on the gap between what's desired and what is. What's desired is baked into the flesh and memories. So long as the gap between what is and what's desired exists, there will be no real peace. This closing of the gap can happen in a couple of ways:

1. Temporarily, through the fulfilling of desires. The desire is sated, but that which creates desire operates just as it always has, and therefore, it creates new desires when old ones are resolved. The juice that comes from getting what you want is temporary. This mode of suffering characterizes human existence, chasing one thing after another. The most successful chasers are still driven by restlessness.

2. Permanently, through surrender. The gap can be closed by surrendering the need for things to be a certain way. This is to fully feel how things actually are without trying to change or resist them. Acceptance is letting it go and forgetting it. This acceptance of feeling drains the energy of that which creates desire, as the thing is built wholly of dissatisfaction. As this energetic thought body weakens, its witness discovers that all the juice of getting one's way is of internal origin, a function of closing the gap. At a certain point, there is the realization that the juice of outside things is illusory and based on nothing more than the loosing of desire's grip on the juice that's already within.

An unhappy person can very quickly come to this realization. Consider the aforementioned gap (desire) to be the height at which the fragile shell of the ego rests. A happy person's ego sits safely close to the ground. For the happy, falling in surrender makes scarcely an impact, as there's little potential energy behind weak desires. However, if the gap is large, like an unrequited love or loss that cannot be easily accepted, it's like a vase that's high up on a shelf. It holds a huge amount of potential energy. To let go of this kind of desire is as the ego's fall from a great height. It will shatter the ego and yield its hidden bounty. Blessed are the poor in spirit.

***

Just as carbon monoxide blocks oxygen from the blood cell, so does identity come between the mirror of the heart and the Love of its witness. Identity has many flavors, but the mechanism of toxicity is the same.

***

Words can point to It, but It blossoms in their absence.

***

The question, "Who am I?" implies that we already realize the mind is not the Self, and yet we seek an answer. If this question is repeated with enough persistence, to the exclusion of thoughts that don't dissipate with the moment they serve, we will get an answer, and it will not be one of words, but freedom, for what we are has no particularization by which it can be bound.

***

Love is not an emotion, as emotions are conditional, but rather, Love is the essence of who we are, though we don't feel our own glow until we surrender to what is and resolve the turbulence of the mind that obscures Love's reflection in the heart.

***

All roads lead to eventual Self discovery, but the outward path is a lesson that, through frustration, tells us what we are not. And in being thwarted in finding fulfillment and/or security in the changeful, we learn that what we seek is the only unchanging thing, which is ourselves, observing all that we once took to be us.

***

If hell is separation from God, then what does belief in the authorship of our thoughts do? If we believe and follow the thoughts that appear in awareness, buy into them as native, though they be denominated in the foreign currency of words, then we believe we possess a will that is in irreconcilable disharmony with the Devine. The thoughts come and go, spun from lower vibrations, and our free will lies in choosing to either believe or "not conceive" that they are both original and represent something that's to be preferred over the moment. In doing so, we establish an imaginary identity on which to hang thoughts deemed personal, an "I" thought, and we give too high an appraisal of its related form and experience. We see it as the "good guy." We hold fear for its loss. So we seek those with a familiar fingerprint of form and experience, as they will have common aims in preserving the superficial. We select a thought-based hell of separation from God and our fellow beings. We are subject only to what we refuse to let go of. In dropping unconscious obedience to vagrant thoughts, we find our true nature.

***

How do I nourish a soul?

Feed it the light of creation by surrendering to what is, turning away from the concept of a desired alternative. Attention given to thoughts disturbs consciousness with their vibrations, which denies the spiritual heart the light of its witness, in whose likeness it would otherwise grow. Your agreement with every moment will put you in harmony with the unfolding of God's will, and in this harmony, the peace of love expands and grows the soul from the spiritual heart. The clay does not question the potter, the knife, nor the wheel, but instead, surrenders to them.

There is a strong inertia to the mind, and we get caught in looping thoughts. The transition between states of consciousness presents a barrier of forgetfulness, like when you fall asleep and don't quite know you're in a dream. That's how it is when the uncontrolled voice dominates. There are many paths, but for some, it takes a persistent and painful disagreement with "what is" to motivate the cultivation of an understanding of how to care for the inner space. Waking up to the mechanics of it reveals the extent to which we're programmed beings. We live in bodies and in circumstances that we don't recall choosing. These things are our karma, and they permeate consciousness as impressions that form a mind, which is also karma. Thought is born of resistance between what is and what's held in mind as the ideal. Surrendering to your karma, surrendering to what is, inwardly, relaxes this resistance and straightens all the lines of tension in consciousness, which allows for the perception of the spiritual heart, from which the soul will grow.

Where there's an inner barrier, there's an inner door. The inner barriers are hidden in plain sight. They are the thoughts that constantly vie for our attention, competing with both each other and the moment. When they connect with attention, there is a vibrational link, and attention nurtures the thought and awareness takes on its vibration. This is why we unconsciously take ourselves to be thoughts, because we take on their vibrations, and all forms are vibration, be they subtle or gross. But we are not the forms; we are the medium through which vibrations make them appear. The vibrations that form matter are born of creation's voice, resonating and moving with the will of the almighty speaker. When we engage the echoes of creation via thoughts, we are playing with the dead and in so doing grow a dead thing within ourselves.

Everything that is vice arises from thought. But the ill created by vice is in the mental illusion it perpetuates, which steals attention from the unfolding of creation, stunting the soul and expanding the rebellious ego. The act is just the vehicle; the driver is the thought that steers it. Stop looking at the vehicle and start looking at the driver. Many people look at commandments on a surface-level, meaning, if an act is defined as ungodly by scriptures, they refrain from carrying it out. Many think themselves sanctified if they take no forbidden actions. But did Jesus ever imply that the Pharisees were sanctified by their adherence to rules? No, actions are just the vehicles, and if you ban one set of vehicles, the world will create another and fill them with the real drivers of spiritual amnesia, idolatrous thoughts.

All concepts should be dropped; all judging should be foregone, all seeking should be turned inward; towards the source of thoughts, where the concept of "I" was born. Find the root of the imaginary person, feel the heart from where arises this idea of an I. The foundation of the person is the "I" thought, and it is a vulnerable thing, being made of thoughts that can be countervailed and being tied to a temporary body. This belief on the part of the permanent, in being founded on the temporary, creates the fear and resistance that hides peace. Love is the absence of fear. In stillness we learn that love is the foundation of our own growth. In the surrendering of our desired alternatives, the disturbance in the heart that's called a mind is stilled, and the heart will reflect its witness. In the light of the creator, the spiritualized atoms of the heart will grow a soul that can be felt. The attention is the light of creation that grows that which it beholds, and so if you give attention to thoughts, which resist God's creation, you will instead grow a demon. The way of the cross is to not fear death, not resist creation, not resist what is, so that the mind will become still, being superseded by the spiritual heart from which grows an angelic soul in the light of God's creation.

***

Imagine the most beautiful being, whose mere glance could bring liberation, but this being lived alone in a world without mirrors, and so the only way they could see themselves was to look in a pool of water, but outside forces would constantly disturb it. They found that if they threw a rock into the pool, its wake would leave a brief patch of smoothness that afforded a temporary clarity for reflection and thus, peace, but overall, the splash would cause more disturbance, brining the need for larger and larger rocks to get shorter and shorter glimpses. The pool is the heart, and the chop is the mind, which arises due to its resistance to outside forces. The rocks are the objects of desire, and the splashes, karma. The being is the Self, seeking ever to apprehend the peace that it is.

***

The phenomenality to which we are witness arises from the One Love we are. This One Love is innocent, having neither form, nor positionality itself, but bearing witness to many forms and relative positions within itself. This innocence believes what it apprehends, and so it reacts to the scenario according to the karma of the form through which it witnesses its expression. Mind is a microcosmic distortion that color's Love's perspective. Attention is a creative faculty within consciousness, and so attention given to retained events makes them grow and permutate, and thus we create our own world. "Others" are expressions of the same Love. They are as characters in your dream, all you from different perspectives within you. There are five sheaths to the body, all movements, mind, which is the retained thought body, gross body, the heart, which is a spiritualized seed that reflects what it holds to its witness, and in the unconscious state, it holds a mind. In the "awakened" state, it is an unblemished mirror that reflects its witness, whose attention grows it in its own true image. The intelligence is of the physical form and interprets according to its capacity, like the CPU on a computer. The energy body facilitates the movements of the other bodies. We are set free by surrendering all resistance to creation, which smooths the mirror of the heart, cleansing it of the mind, and the attention then given this mirror grows it in the likeness of its witness, and thus, the Self is known. Desire is a movement that seeks a stabilizer outside the form, but the movement that seeks creates a distortion that alienates itself from itself, which is suffering. Each desire fulfilled is like a splash in a pool that leaves a temporary stillness in its immediate footprint but that overall creates more distortion in the pool, requiring an even greater splash to make the same stillness. Aversion is just another kind of desire, in that runs from what's not wanted into what is.

***

Desire is a ransom that ego imposes on itself for happiness. The greater the ransom, the more pleasing the payoff, but the ransom is pain in suffering, as it's the imposition of an imagined distance from an unknown source of happiness that is actually our Self. The process also creates an impression, called a Vasana, which is an appetite for more of this reward, a greater intensity. It's what holds us in the pattern of thought-addiction. So the ransom of suffering goes up. There is no steady state here. It's like jumping off higher and higher buildings, only to reach the ground. The ground is happiness, it's just the distance that desire takes you from it that makes a seemingly greater relief.

***

The word gospel means Truth, which is not religion. Religion is a pyramid scheme, telling people to tell people to tell people, ad infinitum. What are you telling them to tell, that believing in a character from a book will magically save them with no real surrender, or that God offers the prosperity which Satan promised Christ in the desert? The mind in which a savior is held is itself a fiction, and the Real will not be found within the false. The same could be said of any character from any book. This won't save anyone. It bestows the blinding certainty of the Pharisee, who thinks the tree of sin is killed by crushing its fruits directly. However, the effect does not precede the cause. Sin and spiritual death are conquered through growing the tree of life. The

Kingdom is in your midst. Not all are ripe for it, and this is why Jesus spoke in parables, and He said as much. Picking up your cross is to surrender to the will of the Father by dissolving the personal will in the spiritual heart where Christ knocks. Find the root of that which rebels against what is, and you will find that it is the "I" thought, out of which grew Adam and Eve's shame. Apprehend who it is that observes this thought by asking, who am I? Turn towards the source of the question and surrender the "I" to this One who truly knows your heart. The fullness of the Spirit comes in surrendering the mind to its observer.

***

How people treat one another has to do with how they see the other through the lens of who they take themselves to be, which is all form and conditioning, nothing more than genetic information and programming, both arising from the causal chain. A high percentage of this programming comes from screens, pages, pundits, and teachers, a small number of homogenizing and polarizing voices that themselves hail from hemmed-in perspectives, the unreal cultivating the unreal from the dross of imagined time. This leaves little room to be informed by this very moment, but the moment is what reveals Truth, not the placeholder of cultivated identity, of dead memory, born of relative truths. Those who dwell in history are doomed to repeat it from alternating sides of the bloodletting cycle, but those who drop time know the peace of who they are.

***

"But we seem to be bound by certain limiting factors."

Be that as it may, there's discovery in discerning which illusions must be given loyalty and which not. As you go through this inventory, you'll find there's a little surrender in seeing that ghosts can not only die but that they lived only through our attention. If the elements of identity are indeed woven from the fabric of imagination, why give them any energetic attention? They are like gas burned in neutral, having no moment to serve. In unloading these concepts, at first it's the unpleasant ones, as there's impetus, but with each concept and thought removed, a little more space is created, and in its place is the space called Love. Soon you realize that the apprehension of the space left by a thought-un-manifested is more rewarding than the taste of the thought-foregone. Through the surrendering of all that resists Now, we know ourselves as the Love we've been using to create middle-men for it. Find the "I" thought that arises from the spiritual heart. Turn it on itself by asking the question, "who am I?" When a thought comes, ask, "to whom does this thought arise?" Treat them all like wrong numbers, unless they have legitimate business:

Thought: "we need to do housework"

Seer: "I'll put you on the calendar. Good bye"

Thought: "that guy looks like a jerk."

Seer: "you have the wrong number." "to whom does this arise?" "Who am I?"

***

Who embodies the Truth is in surrender to it.

***

To a Friend in Doubt

It's not really about understanding so much as dropping all concepts. That's what surrender is about. There's something in each of us that's a point through which the reflection of source can be felt as a very palpable and unconditional peace and love. It's a Love that's not directed at any particular thing but shines in all directions, like the sun. It's the spiritual heart of every being, which reflects the true Self of everyone when the mind that disturbs its surface has been resolved into stillness. It's always there, but it's hidden by the thought-based identity that we call the mind. The mind has its root in a single thought called "I." The I-thought appeared to the child as a way to facilitate relational thinking in a world of apparent duality. There's "I" and "other." On top of this "I," conditioning added a fingerprint of conceptual identifiers that correlate to form and circumstances, e.g., bodily differences, race, culture, belief, nationality, education, opinions, etc. All of these concepts with which consciousness identifies in the "hemmed in" state of identification, belong to time. They are vulnerable.

Belief that we are this subset of things and not the consciousness that witnessed their formation, creates fear. Fear is a lower vibration that masks the aforementioned Love. Additionally, in believing that we are temporal, we seek security, but no amount of security can prevent the inevitable end of every observable thing; therefore, the quest to permanently bring circumstances into alignment with the desire for security is impossible.

Peace can be felt only in the absence of fear. Ideal circumstances can make us feel good and secure for a time, but we wrongly believe the source of the good feelings to be within the trappings of the circumstances, but the feeling can go away even when things haven't changed, e.g., boredom or a fearful idea that randomly appears.

So peace is revealed by the alignment of what's desired with what is, and it can be done from either side, i.e., make the world the way "I" wants it or bring what "I wants" into alignment with the way the world is, to surrender to it. Of the two ways, only one can be sustained, which is the latter, and the path to that place is surrender. Feel what is, accept it, and let it go. All lingering thoughts are resistant to the moment in that they would otherwise dissolve if they served it. The moment is "what is," which has its source in the aforementioned heart. To resist "what is" is to resist the extension of your true Self. You cannot fully know what you resist. Faith is trusting that the reward of this peace is worthy of surrendering and letting go of what are truly imaginary things. You owe no loyalty to the imaginary.

***

When the concept of self shrinks within its shell of insularity, the reality of Self expands in its place. The concept dwindles as melting ice on the vast ocean. The ice has many shapes and levels of clarity, but it's all the same water of Self underneath.

***

When the situation seems bad, there is impetus to do something. You can do something outward, which is what has been done since the beginning, which keeps things going. Everything we resist is the product of other resistance. Consider the worst

111

possible thing about your situation and surrender to it, feel it for all it's worth. Fully feel all that shit and instead of resisting it with the mental protagonist, surrender to it and then just let it go. Give it over to the universe. As it departs, it will take something with it, something that's a blockage to the foundational peace that is your true and hidden nature.

***

Peace and thought are mutually exclusive. The mind is thought. To have permanent peace, the root of the mind must be surrendered to what is, which is the heart. Feel the emotions behind your thoughts and dissolve them into your heart. Find from where the concept of "I" arises inside and merge "I" back to this source, the heart. This is just an adjustment to your "internal posture," but it changes everything if you can stand to part with imaginary things.

***

Were the Absolute an ocean, we would be water balloons, the flesh being our latex. The water would be consciousness, and the air bubbles we hold would be stories, opinions, positions, likes, dislikes, grudges, hopes, regrets, attachments, and fears, i.e., our self-concept and all the things on which we ruminate. The saints would be those without bubbles, pure consciousness in a form. They are neutrally-buoyant, well beneath the waves of the world, feeling only the love they know they are. The superficial chop does not move them at all, only the deep ocean currents can command them.

The wicked have almost no water. Instead they hold mostly air, being full of fears, desires, and self-image. They sit on the surface, blown up with thoughts. They are bounced around by every little disturbance, searching in-vain for an anchor on a sea of change. They cannot feel the ocean beneath, nor its deep currents. They can't feel the existence of the ocean, much less its depths.

Surrender is to let go of some air. When this happens, we feel it, and it is good. If we are fortunate enough to hold enough angst to surrender, we'll make the connection and see that all thoughts separate us from the peace of the Absolute. We'll then proceed to let it all go, not just the "bad," but all of it, even the most cherished ideas. You are subject only to what you believe, for you are always even that from which you feel separation. Blessed are the poor in spirit.

***

Peace is the Self.

The apparent size of the heart is limited only by the words that disguise it, but in Truth, it is utterly boundless.

The sage's bounty lies in the space between words.

The words of the sage work towards the undoing of words, such that the One they hide can be revealed. Who's hidden in your midst has been given many names by many people, but He is always the same. There is but a single heart, and It is revealed in silence. Nothing that aims to reveal this can be heresy or blasphemy, for silence is the noblest end, and it cannot be out of alignment with the spiritual heart.

***

Peace is not even possible until:

1. You decide that peace is actually what you want, rather than struggle or illusion.

2. You realize that because the world constantly changes, it will never hold still for "your" peace, and thus, the direction you must face is inward, not outward.

3. That what disturbs is the very desire to hold both peace and an imaginary identity. The imaginary person whom the child accepted fears and resists everything that seems to oppose it. The two are mutually-exclusive. You can have peace and no person or a person and no peace. But if you want to be a person, it will fight until the day it dies, and no matter how many enemies it kills, there will be another.

***

The barrier between faiths is the same as that which hides God from all seekers. It's the disturbance of thoughts that obscures the heart where God awaits, and likewise, it's the fabric of thought that divides the sects. When one person looks up at the sky, the sun they see through the clouds is not different from that which is seen by another.

Likewise, when stillness of consciousness reveals the heart, the One Who's found is the same, regardless of the name given. God owns all hearts. "Be still and know that I am God." The same stillness will reveal the same God, regardless of the name by which He's identified. For what is anything named in the midst of utter silence?

God knocks on the door to all hearts, but the heart is hidden behind the thoughts that separate us. To whom is this call to silence blasphemy? That one has yet to discover for only having thought and talked and never having devotedly listened to silence. All they know of God is denominated in the very thoughts that hide Him.

***

A Practice for the Christian

Those who would debate about God are as drowning men who refuse to get out of the water, for the water of thought itself hides that which the seeker seeks, for there are no good men, no not one. But when you take stock of what's lacking in a man, it's not his physical body, for that is but a tool with no will of its own. No, it's the mind that holds desires that turn one in the wrong direction. This mind was formed from words in full view of the child whom Christ said we must become. It's that mind who must be crucified.

Talking and thinking are the province of the Pharisees, and Spirit is that of the disciple, but the latter is revealed in none but silence. Instead of debating, try this today, and if you fail, keep trying, this day and each day thereafter, and keep doing it until the fire in your heart literally feels as that which the disciples described when they encountered the risen Christ on the road to Emmaus, for if you don't feel this perpetually, you have not known the fullness of the Holy Spirit.

The person who must be crucified is not made of flesh, but rather concepts. When Christ spoke of plucking out offending body parts, He was not speaking of inanimate flesh, but rather, the mind for whom that flesh is but an instrument.

Silent agreement with creation is surrender to God. Do not try to change the world, but rather, yourself. Every time a thought arises, such that it does not dissipate with an action that served the moment, instead of giving it the floor of your being, turn away from it and give your attention instead to the spiritual heart that lies not with the physical heart, but rather, on the opposite side of the chest. This is the spiritual heart, of which the disciples spoke.

Instead of letting this noise of a thought be heard within, feel your spiritual heart; give it your attention, and crush the thought with an inner "amen," which is your surrender to that which the thought resists. And do this with every thought, and just don't let up on it. As the mind withers in the face of it, the witness of creation will know the burning of the spiritual heart. Know that the old bottle will not immediately be fit for this new spiritual wine, and so there will be discomfort that causes you to change your ways or burst. And some of the thoughts will not be pleasant, and turning to feel the spiritual heart with an "amen," will force you to feel the emotions that underlie these thoughts. Feel them and turn them over to God, and the words that try to spring from them will leave you as well. You can hold none of these grudges while being filled with the Holy Spirit, for He will chastise you. But when you surrender, you will know the water that quenches all thirst. This is the crucifixion of the mind, of the lower self.

***

That which we hold to be "something" is just nothing that veils the connection to everything.

***

The best thoughts are like disposable plates, used once and thrown out. The worst are like fine China, cherished in a display case, beheld every day but seldom used to serve.

***

The intelligence manifests in the form that arises from consciousness. The conditioning is retained in the form as well. The two work in concert as data and processor, but their Knowing is the consciousness that observes them, from which they arose.

***

If God instructed the saint and the Pharisee to not drive to certain places, neither would be seen there. However, the Pharisee would drive by, but never to them. This means they would think of things but not do them. The saint, on the other hand, would have removed the tires from the car and burned them with the gas he siphoned from the tank. This means the saint destroys the root of all thoughts, with the very energy from which they arise. The saint surrenders the mind that is the vehicle for resistance to the perfect unfolding of creation.

***

God, whatever your conception may be, is the uncaused first cause. What appears is not merely born of what immediately preceded it, but rather, the whole of creation. As such, your control of it is an illusion. The death that was promised with the eating of the fruit of the knowledge of good and evil is not merely a physical death but a spiritual one. The spiritual death is also not caused by mere actions, but rather, an inability to grow in the Spirit. It is the death of a stunted seed. But still there exists the opportunity to grow this seed in surrender to the light of creation. Surrender to the Father's will; this is Jesus' example, and indeed, the example of all true saints.

***

Creation unfolds perfectly according to God's will, and to grow spiritually requires no more than the ability to bask the soul in the pure light of it, which is the truth of the moment, unhidden by the editorial thoughts that resist it. It is simply the ability to expose creation's witness to the truth of the moment, without the clouds of thought to shade it. The clouds that hide the nourishing light of creation are just lingering thoughts. Such thoughts always stand in judgement-of and resistance-to creation, else they would dissipate with the moment they serve. The ability to have these resisting thoughts is the fruit of the knowledge of good and evil. It is the ability to hide from the light of creation by constantly thinking of desired alternatives.

The ego is the cloud that hides the light that would otherwise grow the soul. To dissipate these clouds, one must surrender wholly to the perfection of "what is," which is acquiescence to the moment born of God's will. The root of the ego is the "I" thought, and by surrendering it to the spiritual heart, it is dissolved.

The weed of the false light cannot grow without a root. The true light of Now shines on the spirit in silence, and there is no mistaking its growth, for it is not denominated in thought, which is not truth, but rather, peace, which grows from none but the unadulterated moment.

***

The seeker hides the bounty.

That which points outward to peace is what hides it within.

In the play of life, You are not a character but the audience.

If you know life as a play with no characters and an audience of One, then there can be no protagonist or antagonist and no stake in the outcome.

That which ultimately sees, does not change, but that which is seen, does.

***

Surrendering perspective is like giving up one to gain all.

***

Happiness is who we are; unhappiness is just happiness looking for itself in the illusion of something else.

***

Happiness is as conditional to outcome as your reflection is to what you put over your face. You're always there, regardless of what hides it. Dependence on outcome just makes it conditional upon bending the world to the mind's desires, but it's easier and more sustainable to surrender our desires to what is. It's the alignment of the two that reveals happiness, regardless of the actual circumstance.

***

You are what is, but to know the peace of It, you must come into harmony with its unfolding. This is to drop the vibrational drag of thought and unfold in alignment with creation. The surrender to what is reveals the heart in which the I that resists is dissolved. This is by feel and not by thought, for thought hides love's reflection in the heart.

***

The mental dross from which desires arise, hides the true source of what they strive to capture. Surrendering to the reality of their frustration makes palpable the spiritual heart. In this discovery, the I thought that is the root of desires can be dissolved in the heart, and thus, the true and hidden objective is revealed in repose.

***

In the absence of resistance there is no person, as there are no thoughts to resist, and the person is woven of thoughts.

***

No imagined moment can match the prize of this one, regardless of the apparent gulf in desirability. The true prize of the moment does not change with circumstance, even the one that sees the destruction of the flesh. All it takes is unconditional alignment with what is. This is Self-recognition.

***

This Love cannot be known to the thinker that hides It, but faith believes It to be worthy of surrender to what is.

***

The person is a thought-based character, a construct that both hides and seeks the Love who observes it. The person doesn't appear in the absence of thought, and thought doesn't appear in the absence of imagined-moments. A thought-observed refuses to serve the moment in which it arises, else it would pass unseen into manifestation as electricity into an appliance. In lingering, a thought holds attention that would otherwise bask in Love's reflection in the heart.

***

Attacking sin directly through the will's resistance is like crushing the fruit in the hope that the tree will die. It's the surrender of resistance to Now, combined with the leavening of devotion to the heart, that grows the tree of life.

***

Vows are like drawing up a blueprint for a building that's already built. The true path is a demolition via perpetual surrender to what is. Then the adherence to the vows is possible and not a matter of will.

***

Knowing when to let it be

"Do not give dogs what is sacred; do not throw your pearls to pigs. If you do, they may trample them under their feet, and turn and tear you to pieces." Matthew 7:6

Peace entails letting people be in resistance. Though one man clings to the hope of what isn't and pays the price of his ignorance, the other man who sees him, in order to stay in alignment with what is, will accept the other's ignorance as the Father's will until he is ripe to be righted. For to be in resistance to the other's resistance is also resistance.

"All things have been committed to me by my Father. No one knows the Son except the Father, and no one knows the Father except the Son and those to whom the Son chooses to reveal him." Matthew 11:27

***

The content of a good memory that holds us to the past, also brought our attention to the present when it was new. But the reason we feel nostalgic in its recollection and not truly joyful is that the memory is devoid of that which actually held its joy, that being the Truth of the present.

***

The bound, outwardly-chase their own light in the wrong direction, believing the projection that is the gross to be more vibrant than the source that is the Spirit.

They desire the Real, while perhaps never having been fully in the moment of it, save for the childhood-state forgotten.

They attribute a moment's beauty to the experience and not its Truth, never having felt its glow in the absence of an arousing circumstance.

The reality they profess to be the Truth is the one from which they hide in the folds of the mind, creating instead a painful tension between what is and what's desired.

Boredom is the exclusive domain of the mind. Boredom is the mind guarding against being turned in on itself and cannibalized in the heart. It won't let you be still and do that.

The bound jump ahead to dream and fall behind to mourn the expiration of a circumstance that once coaxed them into the moment.

They are never in the moment for pilferage of attention by the ghosts of the mind, who devour the energy poured into them at the expense of spiritual growth.

The expansion into awareness is the transmutation of mind to heart through surrender to what is. All the lines of tension between the inner and outer have relaxed, allowing for the observer to shine its light into the now-still spiritual heart, which grows in its likeness and reflects its peace.

The bound has yet to turn fully to the moment and taste the brightness of their own source, unreflected by memory. The flower of peace grows in the light that's reflected by the pure heart that accepts the mind's surrender.

The liberated has surrendered the mind by the root "I" thought, holding it and turning it in on itself so that it can get no energy. It then cannot resurrect the content it wants to use as bait.

Your attention is a creative faculty, and turning the parasite mind on itself starves it of that fuel. The mind's footprint in the heart shrinks, allowing the light of its witness to nurture and grow it. Turn towards the unchanging witness.

***

To live and see no others is to give and see no takers.

***

What's commonly referred to as love is the glimpse people catch of themselves, reflected off another who has liberated their attention from the mind they take themselves to be. It's a temporary state that persists so long as the attention can be held. But the source of that reflection is eternal.

***

The Troubled Village

Once there was a village that was at war with itself over the merits of having either the left or right nostril clogged, until one day a great teacher came and taught the people how to blow their noses.

The part resists the whole until surrender to their mutual source reveals unity.

The disturbed part will never overcome the disturbing whole, but in its surrender to their mutual source, there is peace.

When the will of the of the illusory doer is believed over the will of creation, it is suffering. When the Will of creation is surrendered-to entirely, it is the Truth that reveals Peace.

***

The voice that implores one to fix the world is also heeded by the one who appears to be breaking it. A cancerous cell cannot cure the cancer of other cells but must first heal itself. It's resistance on the part of all divided minds, to the One mind of creation, that brings the apparent problems to the world, as every perspective works towards a different end that it believes is correct, but some are mutually-exclusive. But that refuses surrender to what is will yield anything but suffering.

***

Energy never goes away; it just changes form between cause and effect. Each person you encounter is an extension of the very first cause, even if their form cannot knowingly confess it. See the source in them and thus, know your Self.

***

The thing inside that gets offended, it is not the heart, but rather, that which is displaced BY the heart in surrender to the perfect unfolding of the universe.

The peace of the Self is apprehended in the space between thoughts. Surrender to what is allows it. The ills we resist are born of resistance.

Knowledge of Self is not denominated in thought, but rather, silence. Peace is inverse to thought.

Your natural state eclipses the product of desire. That's why a single taste of it can forever quench the thirst.

***

The thing that offends is ego, and the thing that gets offended is ego. The thing that can neither rightly-offend nor be offended, is the heart. Neither side of cultural conflict has experiential knowledge of the heart, just periodic flashes of happiness that occur when the moment temporarily aligns with the desires of the mind. The mind is resistance that hides the heart, because the heart is actually everything there is, and by rejecting any part of it, its true nature cannot be apprehended. These combatants will never, ever, be able to bring the universe into permanent alignment with their desires, not even with a holocaust of those they despise; therefore, the heart will remain hidden to them until they surrender their desires to the perfect unfolding of the universe. It's none but the sleeper who struggles with the dream, but the lucid, by accepting without condition, embodies love without condition.

***

How you think determines how you feel, but no thought resonates higher than the heart-space it disturbs. No thought vibrates higher than "no thought."

***

The joy of what can be had or done comes from the temporary alignment of the mind and the moment, but the thought of them breaks the alignment. Surrendering the "I" of the mind to the heart opens this door without condition.

The object of desire has no permanent reward because desire itself closes the door to Self knowledge.

So long as the identity is believed, the Self is unknown.

Belief in anything hides the knowledge of God, which is not denominated in thought. When Christ comes into your heart, you are dissolved in His.

Presence, is surrender-to and agreement-with your Self, such that It is not obscured by the argument of thought.

***

Peace is revealed in surrendering the perception of imperfection.

***

The individuated consciousness is as a bolt, the shape and threads of which are forged from experience. The threads are the mind that grabs a hold of things. The torque of desire can over-tighten and strip these threads, such that the futility of further turns is realized. It then becomes still. So long as the threads of conditioning remain robust, desire will hold it to the machine, but a stripped bolt will be surrendered to its source, defined not by form, but rather, the metal it always was.

***

The inner voice that says "resist," said the same to the one you resist, from a different, but no-less arbitrarily-assigned position. But for the illusion created by form and perspective, they are you, consciousness heeding a voice that relates to a part of the causal chain. If you want it to stop, stop heeding the voice. Stop trying to fix everything. The voice that causes the problems is the sum of all resistance to Now. See perfection in the unfolding, surrender to what is, without editorial, and the true nature of Peace will reveal Itself.

***

Desire

Surrender wholly to the reality of not getting the most-coveted vessel, and instead, you'll get what you believed it contained.

***

Lucid Dreaming

The sleeper forgets themselves in the night's dream because what they take themselves to be in the day becomes the world in which they dwell at night. In viewing their thoughts as a world instead of wearing them as an identity, they are more truly themselves, but since they are not acquainted with their true Self in waking, they don't know who they are in the dream. In dropping the thought body during the day, they learn their true identity and thus, do not forget It when they sleep.

***

The Hidden Message of the Bible

The mind itself is the fruit of the knowledge of good and evil. It is the accumulated product of the faculty of measurement between what is, which is God's will, and what's desired as the ideal, which is not. This is why Adam and Eve felt shame at the nakedness in which they were created and hid themselves, diverging from God's ideal. This mass of "good" alternatives we hold in mind, stands between creation and its witness, and reflects what we call an identity, which is the false self that brings division and strife. Perpetual surrender to the will of the Father, which is "what is," is the way of the cross.

Jesus demonstrated this time and time again, e.g., in the desert, by rejecting the world, in the garden of Gethsemane, when He allowed His arrest, as He stood before Pilate, and ultimately, on the hill of Golgotha. He accepted the cup and rejected the alternatives.

When "you" perpetually surrender to what is, by feeling and not resisting or reacting-to the emotional product of both thoughts that arise, as well as the moment itself, you are following Christ's example, and the illusory veil of mind that stands between creation and its witness begins to thin. As this progresses, the spiritual heart becomes palpable, and what is felt is none other than the Spirit of Truth, for in holding the root of the mind, i.e., your undivided attention, to the spiritual heart, the mind is dissolved. What is perpetually felt in this surrender is the very water of which Christ spoke to the Samaritan woman at the well.

The mind is life's accumulation of thoughts that idealize all but the moment (God's will), and the accumulated mind hides the child Christ said we must become to be with Him. When the mind is seen as false through its dissolving in the heart, the fruit of the Spirit is manifested within, and all desires are killed. The fruit of the Spirit is the contentment He brings. The fruit of the Spirit is the unity that comes in the surrender of circumstantial individuation, i.e., the thoughts you take yourself to be, e.g., race, politics, culture, traditions, opinions, likes, dislikes. You are not these things, but rather, their witness. The body of Christ is this One you know yourself to truly be. The fruit of the Spirit is the selfless act that arises from the lack of self and knowledge of Self.

The God that's held in mind as a thought is an idol, and it is held in mind by so many that the way is narrow. The prosperity preachers are the devil in the desert, for their reward is one and the same. The identity pushers are the serpent in the garden, selling you an imaginary character instead of its witness. You are not your thoughts, nor the physical form! The Kingdom is in your midst!

***

Some air was trapped in a dense log. Wood was its only view, and so it reasoned, " I'm bound by my wooden frame." Then the log rolled into the water, and being dense Mopani, it sank to the bottom. The air became a bubble in the log and reasoned, "this water that swirls in my frame colors my view, and it holds oxygen, and so it is me too. Seeing only wood and water but never air, it eventually forgot that it was a bubble. One day the currents pushed the log over the edge of a deep chasm. As it sank, the pressure of the water began to crush the bubble in a most uncomfortable way. The pain made it realize that it was not the water that was crushing it, and the weight-difference between itself and the heavier

129

water created a strong upward pull. When the pull and pressure were too great, it let go of the log and began to ascend, giving in to the forces around it. As it headed upwards, it could feel itself expanding as the water pressure diminished. Larger and larger it grew, until it broke the surface and became one with the atmosphere. Then it knew itself as all air.

***

What you take yourself to be is a story that diverges from what is. Surrender that story and realize that you are the screen on which it plays out.

***

The Truth sees what arises from Itself, including the window through which It's observed.

Does the skin cell know what it is? And yet it contains the blueprint for the whole being.

What is apparent arises from the Truth. Resistance doesn't change It, just obscures It.

***

The shadow is cast upon those do not fall within the protagonist's perspective.

The cultivation of identity is the lullaby that renders unconsciousness. Identity is conceptual, the stuff from which the blanket of forgetfulness is woven. How can there be Self-knowledge when we heed the siren song of "I'm proud to be of this race, gender, orientation, nationality, political party, tribe, fan club, etc.?" There is today, a major news site that has subsections for specific identities. It's not that a particular identity is to blame, it's that identity is itself an impediment to Self-knowledge.

***

Just as leaves arise from the tree but are not the wood, thoughts and forms arise from the Truth but are not the Truth. For the Truth is unchanging, and leaves come and go, but the wood does not. Who can see the wood when standing beyond the canopy that's thick with leaves? You can circle the tree and stand in every possible perspective and still not see the wood through the leaves. But if you can get close in, behind the leaves, the tree will reveal itself.

***

The joy that comes from acquisition and experience is as the sunlight reflected from a mirror. This light can be seen only when attention is given to that mirror, which ever-precludes turning towards its source to see the true light. The source of the joy that's temporarily reflected off worldly attractions is the heart's witness, but those mirrors give only distorted light and are effective only so long as they hold novelty and thus, attention.

For one who constantly looks outward, the quest never ends, as the means to that quest is thought, which clouds and obscures the heart. But when the true light is reflected from the heart, the clouds of thought are as poison, and there is no choice but to remain focused on the heart. "Blessed are the poor in spirit, for theirs is the kingdom of heaven." Matthew 5:3. There is motivation to surrender painful thoughts but very little when they are as sweet poison.

***

When it's seen that action arises still from silence, and that the worded thoughts are redundant, the illusion of the doer dissolves.

***

131

The mind is the big secret. Its existence is believed when its nature is unknown. It doesn't really exist, because it is imaginary, and to personify it is a falsehood. And yet, it seems to be real, like Pinocchio, but it is an echo that bounces around in a structure that arises from its witness.

The mind is not real; it is merely regarded as such by the medium through which it resonates when given the creative light of attention.

The mind is not conscious of itself, as it is a mere movement, but because it is being expressed by something that can see nothing but its own manifestation, its source takes that to be itself, because it is otherwise nothing but a space.

In the absence of movement in this space, it reverts to its own nature, which is peace. To still the space requires the agreement of the thoughts with what is, such that they disappear. Thoughts are cumulatively the mind, and their source is the heart. Surrender the mind to its source.

***

Lucidity is to be so in the moment that the will is surrendered to the unfolding of creation. The creation is within the creator, and agreement with the Author's intelligence is Self-knowledge.

***

See the world as perfect because that is real change. It's resistance that creates what you resist. No movement can predate the space it occupies; therefore, the space is the first cause, the Absolute. The effect is the cause transformed, for energy is never lost. As such, the space can see itself in movements stemming directly from its will; however, it does not recognize itself in the echoes that lag, resist, or extrapolate-from it. These are thoughts, distortions that obscure the moment with counterfeit overlays. This is why Self knowledge depends upon silent agreement with the will that drives the moment.

The echoes must be resolved, surrendered to the moment from which they arose, no matter how correct they appear. This is to give them up to the heart. The fruit of fulfilled desires arises not from the experience but rather, its temporary agreement with the moment. The quest to align the real and imagined, by changing the former, is painful, unending, and yields only partial and temporary peace, but surrender brings the peace of agreement permanently, completely, and effortlessly. Surrender is a matter of allowing the feelings and letting them go, so as to stay present. Resistance is to hold an unresolved idea that precludes presence, and thus, Self knowledge. It's grace that highlights the inequality between surrender and resistance. See the world as perfect.

***

If you resist it, you believe it, if you believe it, there's a you to believe it. Belief in the character precludes knowledge of its source.

***

It's a big briar patch. We're in its midst so long as we draw breath. Some have found the space between the thorns by surrendering into them for release, while others pull against them, ensnaring themselves deeper, tugging at the thorns of those stuck in the same branches.

Creatively show people how to see the superficial for what it is. Show them the mind by describing it, as a witness does to a sketch artist. Show them the imaginary and counterfeit nature of its fabric. Show them the folly of loyalty to form and conditioning, how it's born of a long chain that merges back to one source that claims parentage to all that moves through it.

All appearances are cracks in the same fracture, but really, we're not the cracks but the glass through which they run. Why should one despise another? The source is one with its expression. It is contiguous to all forms and knows their perspectives in the only way that's fair, first person.

***

There is Nothing to Lose

Identity is a movement in consciousness that's sustained by attachment to form and experience. It is like a fingerprint, unique to the divided mind. The witness of the identity identifies with it, because it is otherwise without form, and so it holds to what it has apparently become. It knows that the objects of attachment belong to time, and so its attachment to the temporal is the root of fear. Fear hides the love through which it moves. Identity is a vibrational fingerprint that captivates its witness; therefore, the captive wants to be surrounded by likeness. Dissonance brings destructive interference that inflames it. It fears the other. Identity is the source of hate, but it is entirely imaginary. Hate will never be resolved through deeper pride in the identity. This is the folly of I, the illusion that attachment to identity brings anything but more hate. The resolution of this glorified thought, the "I," reveals love and dispels hate.

The "I" cannot live wholly in the moment because Now has no memory, and the I is past. Hate requires attachment, which requires memory, which is again, precluded by presence. The root of identity is the "I" thought on which all concepts hang. The "I" thought can be isolated by the repeating of its name, "I, I....". Then there is no thought but the I, and in such repose, the heart from which I arises can be felt, for feeling is inverse to thinking. Drop the I into the heart from which it arose, and it will eventually dissolve. This is called surrender to the true Self, which is the space through which I moves. This is to wholly accept "what is," in the same manner as the I was once accepted, but since "what is" survives all change, there is no fear of losing it. It is Love. Then Love knows Itself as the medium through which I once moved.

***

The Holy Spirit is the spirit of Truth, and what is Truth but what is? To what did Christ surrender when He allowed the crucifixion? What is The Father's will but what is? The thought taken to be a self is the lie, and the moment it resists is the Truth. Surrendering the lie to the truth is submission to the will of The Father and the end of desire, of suffering.

***

If it entails anything but dropping it, drop it.

***

Any thing considered essential to freedom is a roadblock until it's surrendered.

***

To even oppose the resistance of others is resistance. The ego is not conscious and not real. It is an observed phenomenon playing out, and so like a falling tree limb, it should not be taken personally, regardless of the vantage point from which it's seen. Its fictional composition is given meaning through personalization, when nothing believes a declaration that it owns something, a body, an identity, memories, and objects. Peel each away and there remains what believed it was that. But to abdicate claim to these while still amidst their unfolding, that is freedom.

***

The heart's testimony is completeness that's revealed in silence.

***

The teacher you can see can do nothing more than introduce the teacher you can feel.

***

Faith is the impetus to pursue a knowledge that is not denominated in thought and seek a reward that has no worldly form.

***

We're in the prison of identity and fighting over who has the better cell. Kill the guards and escape.

***

There is a mode of existence that goes beyond the five senses. You can tell someone about it, but their knowing of it is a solo endeavor. The believer doesn't know it but says it exists via a personified entity that can grant it. The atheist also doesn't know it but says it doesn't exist.

The unknowing believer lacks Self-knowledge, being wrong about who they are and extending this error to the One after whom they believe themselves to be patterned.

The unknowing atheist also lacks Self-knowledge, believing him or herself to be limited to form and perspective.

The person is a shell that holds this miracle, and the Knower is no person at all. Break open your inner construct and find the nectar.

***

Disgust points not to an outer problem, but an inner blockage.

Desires are eclipsed in the dropping of aversions. This doesn't necessarily mean that you do all aversions, but rather, accept them as having also arisen from the source of what you unconsciously take yourself to be. You cannot know your source, and thus, your Self, while rejecting any part of its product. What reacts to the product of your source is what hides it. Disgust calls out from the inner falsehood, and so the object of disgust is telling you what must be surrendered to the heart.

***

That from which words arise is beyond their ability to describe.

***

What you despise the most, that is your guru. When you surrender to it and see through the illusion of the you who was once believed to be above it, you will dissolve into freedom.

***

The first decade passes slowly for the child. Life seems to accelerate with age, and it's because attention given to now shrinks relative to immersion in dead memory, as attention is a zero-sum-game. The halls of memory are a thief of life. Children have no chronological corpse to steal their moments. Presence bestows the fullness of living.

***

In the revelation of Self, the words used to guide are disposable.

***

If animals live in the moment, why is it said that we "live like animals when we do not?"

The creative capacity that animals lack is also that which deludes us. In the roller coaster of Maya, humans can create and climb the hill of illusion that allows the plunge into Self-realization. Animals stay at the bottom, already in the garden, unable to leave it, forget it, then get back in through surrender. You have to be able to "sleep" and dream vertically to wake up. When man lives "like an animal," he's not chasing the same thing as the animal. The animal chases to satiate the body's urgings but knows true peace when physically satiated. Man unknowingly chases to escape the dream, which no amount of getting will permit, for the novelty of acquisition is but a temporary exit from the mind that does not reveal the true source of peace. He chases in the wrong direction until he realizes its futility. In surrendering "what's desired" to "what is," the mind is unmasked as the gatekeeper. He goes from wanting it all in the belief of separation, to being it all in the knowledge of Self. We can know the light because we can know the darkness, for we have eaten the fruit of knowledge.

***

No teaching is as profound as the silence to which it points.

The person who would fix the world is a noise that promises the fruits of silence.

The ills we resist are born of resistance.

***

Take a look in the mirror. I don't care who you are; there's a stranger who takes issue with your existence by virtue of any number of supposed reasons, e.g., history, religion, racist ideology, politics, favorite sports team, etc. And by the same token, there are those who identify with your descriptors who feel the same hate for the "other."

False love cannot exist without hate, for their border delineates "mine" from "other." The small self thinks love wins when all is "mine" through suppression or elimination of "other," but True Love undergirds all, playing peekaboo with itself through diverse illusions.

***

The perception that life is passing by, along with the accompanying fear and nostalgia, is optional. If you live in the moment, time doesn't exist. This dropping of thought unshackles awareness, and if done persistently and consistently, there arises a Peace that confesses its identity as your deepest Self.

***

Audible words cannot justly describe what's revealed in the abandonment of those yet unvoiced.

The pain of desire is the product of resistance, but the peace that displaces it is the product of surrender.

***

What we chase is an expression of what we already are. Why chase yourself?

Q: *So that girl I'm chasing is me?*

A: Everything is energy. 99.999999+% of your body's volume is the space between sub-atomic particles, and what isn't space is just a vibration within that space. We are movements within an energy field to which both you and that girl are contiguous. The different forms you see are just different vibrations within the same field. Your form is a vibration-based structure that retains observations as experience, and these accumulated impressions in consciousness form a shell of information that's reflected back to awareness, making it believe that it is a separate thing. When you are perpetually in alignment with the moment, this "thought wall" dissolves, and you palpably know that you are a wave within a conscious singularity, and this is felt as unconditional and unceasing love, bliss, peace. Also, all the temporary good feelings you get from catching what you chase are just derivatives of that feeling of unity that comes with total agreement with "what is," i.e., you hold no thoughts because this moment is valued over any alternative you could hold in mind, at least so long as the newness of the desired object persists. When you get bored, thoughts return and rebuild the "dam" of thoughts that separate perception from the love that you are. Having that girl just lets you unknowingly know yourself for a time, but you don't actually need her if you can stop all thought through surrender to what is.

***

Clarity of consciousness reveals the flavor of thoughts arising to diminish Its vibration. In the absence of thought, awareness knows the Peace of its purity. It is Love, Sat Chit Ananda. But attachments, deep impressions in consciousness, hold stories that are the printing presses of lower thoughts. "He did me an injustice! I want to get back at him!" "He owes me!" "If I could just have him or her or that, then I'd be happy!"

These notions become the mind that burns up when exposed to the moment. That is why it cannot stand Now. It gets bored or frustrated when the moment doesn't match what's held as mind. It needs a token of action to resolve the desire. It fears the bare moment, which will reveal the mind as an imposter.

***

Words are as relevant to realization as the kindling that starts the fire. The evidence of their efficacy is their subsequent absence.

The words that point to Self-knowledge are like kerosene and those that comprise the personal identity, water. Both are liquid, but when thrown on the fire, the former kindles it and vanishes without a trace, while the latter smothers it, permitting no flame until it evaporates.

***

A person who feels their own lovingness is someone who holds only a thin veil of cares, if any at all. That this state, which is the highest fidelity to truth, would be considered sociopathic, is because too few have felt what's there when the backdrop of noise truly starts to fall away. The child to whom Christ calls, that child predates the experiential

141

programming that identifies with a name today. The surrendering of the mental construct of the grownup is the path to becoming this child. It is nothing more than seeing thoughts and saying "I'm not that." And conversely, looking at reality, and saying "I am that," and loving it, and being true to it, never adulterating it with the restlessness of a desired alternative. This fidelity to Truth is what realizes the Spirit of Truth.
***

The notion that unity is born of superficial sameness and agreement of thought is an illusion, as thought and form are the walls that hide the unity from which they arise.
***

Thought precludes the peace it promises.
***

When you are offended or annoyed, you've been blessed with an opportunity to see. Find the thing inside that is bothered, search for it, feel it. When you get your attention wrapped around this offended thing, look for you own heart, and then pull the offended one down into it and feel it dissolve. Keep doing this every time there is a reaction, and the joy that's revealed will eclipse anything that you could possibly be denied.
***

Murder and oppression are not exclusive *an* identity, but are rather, the product of identity itself. Just add power and watch.

Hate is born of the competition fostered by greed, which promises that more security will preserve the temporary that fears destruction. We wave our little flags from behind the thoughts that we take ourselves to be, thinking there's merit to the body and experiences we've been arbitrarily assigned. We cannot see that the fingerprint of identity has no merit. We just want the same thing the "other" wants, which is power... power to bring reality into alignment with our desires, which is one hell of a lot harder, more costly, troublesome, and temporary than approaching it the other way, which is to bring our desires into alignment with what is.

It seems like the world will fall apart if we don't resist and change it, but we've been here for a long time, and what needs to change is us. We need to examine the mind and what it really is. Because the mind unites along conceptual and superficial lines, it is a divider, a fence behind which are mine and beyond which are yours. Unity is in dropping the mind. It can be seen from the space between thoughts and dissolved when surrendered to the heart.

***

To ascend to Love, you must transcend all you love.

***

Unity is in the space between thoughts.

***

The heart of one is the mind of all.

***

Q: *What would I remove from the world?*

A: Nothing, the ills we resist are born of resistance. Greed and hate arise from a resistance to the moment. As we go through life, the mind swirls with thoughts that are out of alignment with "what is." They are always plotting the next move or reflecting on what was, which causes misery that begs for escape.

This is nothing more than resistance to a moment that is deemed "not enough," e.g., not entertaining enough, not secure enough, not loving enough, not fulfilling enough. The past is either regretted, longed-for, or is a source of bitterness. The future is either anticipated or feared. Search yourself, acknowledge and observe this.

***

The ego remains a prison so long as it's invisible. But once its witness can consistently perceive it, a distance can be maintained. Its assertions can be seen as irrelevant, imaginary, and ultimately, it will wither for lack of attention. The harder it tries to get attention, the more its visibility will diminish it. In this escalation, hurtful things will arise, and instead of resisting them, they should be felt in the heart and surrendered there but not dwelled upon. Eventually it becomes nothing more than junk mail.

***

Doing stops when the peace of being eclipses the product of action.

***

The I-doll is the idol.

***

Love's pursuers unknowingly chase themselves in each other, but the chase precludes the catch. A wave will never catch the one it follows, but in surrendering to what the ocean brings, it resolves into itself.

***

Eternity is in the reconciliation of the mind to the moment.

***

Everything cannot be owed anything. The accounts-receivable department supports the fiction that precludes Self-knowledge. Let go of all that isn't, and embrace all that is, which is You.

***

On the Actions of Others

Form and conditioning delineate "you" from "other," but the same Self operates through all. What "we" hate is created by the same Self, and that Self is experiencing its creation from a form and perspective that loves what you hate; therefore, don't judge it, and be free. You would love what you hate if you were granted a different form and perspective.

***

Three Paths

The spiritual seeker, knowingly or unknowingly, seeks knowledge of Self. Self-knowledge is not denominated in thought, but rather, feeling. The Self is the only real thing, the singularity within-which the shifting fabric of the dream swirls. You are It. To find the only real thing requires the ability to discern It from its expression. The thought of it is not It, but rather, the veil that hides It. To feel "what is" requires the recognition and abandonment of the temporal. Three modes of Self-knowledge are surrender, presence, and Self-inquiry. They lead to the same clarity. Surrender is the reconcilement of "what is" to "what's desired" through the shifting of the latter towards the former and not the reverse.

Surrender - The path through which the Self is known is blocked by alternatives that hold attention. They are fears and desires. You are "what is," and

145

fears are a distraction from that by a misguided wish to safeguard it. They are a diversion. Desires aim to change what is through the mental holding of a preferred alternative. Surrender involves feeling the emotions that underlie fears and desires without a reaction or focus on the details. When the feelings are felt and released, the content falls away with them, no longer a distraction. It must be done perpetually as fears and desires arise. Surrender to fear is an acceptance of the impermanent nature of form, so that its source may be apprehended. The surrender to desire is the acceptance of the feeling of having "what is" instead of the thought of its alternative. The thought of the alternative is a blinding hole, but "what is" is a doorway to Self-knowledge, veiled by the particulars of the moment. Regardless of the content, "good" or "bad," "what is" is always the same peace, waiting behind the veil of the phenomenal. Letting go of these by way of feeling is the trading of thinking for feeling. In silence, the Self is known.

Presence - Presence is simply living in the moment, a focus on Now that precludes thought. But the mind that comes between Now and its Witness is strong. It will not be denied through simple will power. It will pull you out of the moment with fear and desire. It must be worn down through surrender and Self inquiry.

Self Inquiry - This is simply a search and finding of the I thought that arose from the spiritual heart of the child. It facilitated relational thinking within the illusion of duality. All identifications that create insularity, hate, and false love hang upon this I thought. Self inquiry searches within for this I and holds to it to the exclusion of all other thoughts. When there is nothing but the feeling of the I, it can be merged back into the now-palpable spiritual heart.

***

Attention is a zero sum game. Inner-feeling is inverse to thinking and outer sensation. Thinking is born of the view that things are not equal, and thus, the thought of one thing can supersede the reality of another. Outer sensation supports the notion that things are unequal. Things taste good, feel good, look good, and so they are deemed worthy of thought. Other things feel bad, and so they call out as hazards for which an avoidance strategy must be contemplated. They call to us from the timeline, and we go to them, and in so doing, we make ourselves partially unavailable to that which requires our whole attention. However, when thought is seen as the source of life's distress, there is impetus to exit it. This exodus into the moment reveals thought to be the destroyer of the reward it purports to deliver. This is evidenced by the palpable feeling of inner-peace in the stillness of mind. The short path is surrender. Surrender to the worst that thoughts have to offer, letting the feelings be felt, without resistance, reaction, or focus on the content, and then let them go. The emotional energy correlated to a thought can be surrendered away, destroying its magnetism to attention. As the lower vibrational thoughts are resolved, the thinning of the veil will be felt within. It will be a sense of well being that seems independent of circumstances. When this Peace is known to be the product of stillness, it's understood that all outward pursuits are middle men who offer only derivatives of this Peace. Then the peace outshines the product of its bane, and things get done just the same. Who ever was the doer?

***

When the illusory protagonist attacks countervailing illusions, they multiply.

In directly attacking the fruits of illusion, the unconscious reinforces the ignorance from which they arise. Ego attacks ego, and in so doing, plants more seeds of conflict. But in discovering and surrendering to the source of that which they fight, the imaginary protagonist dissolves.

***

The delusion that supports oppression is not endemic to the powerful. A lack of power does not confer an abundance of merit.

***

When you see gold and copper on the movie screen, which is more valuable? They are equally worthless as projections on a screen. A projection is a higher dimensional energy seen as a reflection off a lower-dimensional surface. So a three-dimensional light beam becomes an illusion of 3D objects reflecting from a 2D plane (the screen). That 2D plane will be whatever is projected onto to it. In this respect it has unlimited potential, but within the limits of 2D.

Now consider that the space we observe is a 3D surface on which the reality we see is projected from a higher dimension. The medium for this projection is vibration. Subatomic particles are vibrations. The space between those particles comprises very near 100% of your volume. You are nothing, and you are everything. You are that which hosts the vibration being projected onto it, and what appears as you, to you, is just the view from the form that has been given senses by the intelligence of the projector. The local form has also been given the ability to project the wispy vibrations of thought. The retention of these vibrations in consciousness is what gives it the impression that it's a separate thing. It sees these thoughts to be as real as anything else, and it defends them too.

You see from every form according to its way of being. The third dimension splits the expression of consciousness into separate forms that may, if capable, operate from the illusion of personal perspective. Each view is but one aspect of the same consciousness that sees all perspectives unknowingly from the first person. When two fingers are half-submerged in water, they can't see where the hand unites them, and they can't feel the other's joy and pain. If you give them senses, memory, and experience, they will never know of their common body. Only by freeing up the inner sense can the root be discovered. The resistance to what is must be surrendered to unhook the barb of thought. Untethered from thought, attention can know the inner senses and the spiritual heart. The thought of the person must be found and dissolved in this heart. Life is one playing as many. From the seat of the space, the copper and gold are just different forms of the same thing.

***

The root of discord is the illusion that the uniqueness arising from form and position constitutes the whole being and that the particulars of this form and story bestow special merit that warrants advantage over "others." These needs arise from the mind's perception of vulnerability, as forms are temporary, and so it must work ceaselessly for two things, security and novelty of the kind that temporarily stills it by holding attention elsewhere, lest it be seen.

In fact, we are but one consciousness, reacting simultaneously and independently from many forms and positions. The conscious mind can know the mechanics of this array, but so long as consciousness truly believes the apparent separation, the conceptual self will be uncontested in its push to preserve things, all of which are temporary and/or imaginary. This mental defense budget comes at the expense of a foundational peace that is not felt in the vibration of thought.

Sometimes the struggle to resist what is becomes so painful that the circumstances must be surrendered to. If the timeline becomes infested with fears and regrets, surrendering to the moment becomes so sweet a refuge that the mind falls down into the heart. As this progresses, a gap widens between the thought-content and its witness, as the former atrophies from a lack of attention and emotional juice. At this point the mind's scam is over because as it fell into the heart, the peace that accompanied its ebb was noted. Thus the mind is no longer heeded, as the payoff of its pursuits is known to be a function of an inner stillness that can be had without an acquisition or experience.

***

Speculation on the illusions of others is your own illusion disguised as theirs.

***

The "other" is also an expression of consciousness, but they arose from a different position, and so they also suffer the illusion of a personal self that must fight for notions it thinks it embodies. You would be them, given 100% overlap in the circumstantial; so don't judge them. Until the root of the arbitrary persona is identified, apprehended, and surrendered to its source, conflict will feel justified from behind the walls of thought.

***

There are different impressions of what it means to be awakened. In some parlance, it's becoming informed on an issue, an additive process of gaining knowledge, e.g., learning a system. This is to awaken to something. The learner has become enlightened on a topic.

The other kind of awakening is to the unreal, to know the knowable is not the knower, and that these knowable things should therefore not be regarded as the Absolute, for to believe such an illusion is the root of fear, from which all pathology arises. It is also to discover that certain types of perceptions are mutually-exclusive, such as perceiving thoughts and the inner sense that knows the spiritual heart. This sense is not known from within the vibration of thought.

***

151

Discovery can occur when one flavor of pain has been persistent for too long, particularly if it's around a single issue. That one issue is a thought that monopolizes the energy. It turns the ego into a single-celled organism that is easily seen to be the root of pain. When this one thing can be surrendered to completely, it can break the loop of negativity, as an un-diversified body of grievance can be resolved with one solution. It could be exercised by surrendering to its pain and then letting it go, after giving it undivided but non-reactive attention. Surrender can deal a mortal wound to the parasite.

The space that's left in this resolution allows for a control of attention, as the gravitational pull of the negative mass is gone. It also creates a space between the passing thoughts and their witness. This space reveals the impersonal nature of thoughts.

This inner-arrangement can be instructive as the bounty of its discovery unfolds. In this unfoldment, love awakens to itself. This high state reveals all else to be merely derivative. It would be as if one went from having access to none but downstream water to getting it straight from the source. With unlimited access to headwaters, no variation of dirty water will be seriously pursued. Things appear equal, as objects from 15,000 feet.

***

How is the body picked?

Karma picks the body. Karma is the mind, arising from circumstances both upstream and downstream of birth. The expression of consciousness is given variation by the body and mind, but in the absence of these vibrations, consciousness is uniform in stillness. So a being is a vibration. Every form vibrates at a certain level. The pitch is a function of the patina of thoughts clinging to the "I" thought.

The vibration of a being is like a chord, the notes of which are thoughts and emotions given expression by consciousness. These thoughts and emotions are a product of what's held in mind from experience. The vibration of a being changes through life, according to what's held in mind. By the time the body stops, the chain of actions associated with that form has spiderwebbed out through the world, creating other circumstances, one of which will match the vibration that the previous form held upon exit. A being whose karma holds the same vibrational fingerprint as the previous form arises from the circumstances born of that vibration. Karma makes waves that bring consciousness into forms that correspond to its vibration. There are no people; there are forms arising within consciousness from circumstances stemming from a causal chain. People are the embodiment of circumstances being witnessed by one consciousness that has fractalized its attention, identifying with each form according to its circumstances and capacity. A being is liberated when they, while embodied as a form, achieve the stillness in which there is no mind, no karma, and thus no consequence arising from action. In this, consciousness feels its imagined identity slip away as it regains perception of its full scope.

***

Non-duality is the golden rule perfected, for in duality, it will be approached only asymptotically.

***

153

Thoughts give us feelings, but have we stopped thinking long enough to know how we would feel in their absence? There is an energetic emotional body within each being. It is vibration through the medium of consciousness. The vibrational level is set by the thought content that resonates through this energy body. If a person has a strong belief that they are the body and unconsciously accepts their thoughts as a personal identity, their state of being will hinge upon the state of thought.

The thought body is not only fearful for the loss of its vehicle, the physical body, but it is also under the impression that it must defend its opinions, as if dissent posed a mortal danger.

There is an inertia to this mass. It's like a shark that has to keep swimming, lest it be seen or drown. When there is longstanding acceptance of thought, a thought-stoppage is prevented by the vibrational inertia of the energy body. Negative thoughts leave low vibrations that attract more negative thoughts. A gap in thinking is just an unnoticed slowdown in the traffic. But such a low vibration does call out for relief, in activities that are fodder for more low vibrational thoughts, be they nostalgia for the pleasant or anger for the unpleasant. Pursuit of acquisition and experience is a temporary respite that perpetuates the status quo, like scratching an itch.

***

How do I keep this feeling of love?

It's a matter of surrendering to what is. The disturbance that hides Love is thought, but we forget, just like we forget who we are in the dream. So long as thoughts vibrate through consciousness by way of the attention given them, there's less alignment with Love. Resistance creates these distortions, thoughts. Thoughts confess resistance to the moment, else they would be redundant, and thus, invisible. There is a line of tension between what is and what's held in mind as the ideal, and from this tension arises the fog of dissonance that hides Love. The temporal feeling of love happens when we achieve a one-pointed mind. The lack of a mind leaves us totally in the moment, which is stillness that reveals Love as everything.

When you're in love, it's your own Love that you're feeling, because there is only one Love. Its glow emerges in silence, stillness, and equanimity. It cannot give loyalty to your personal thoughts because it knows no provincialism. It's the same in everyone, and everyone is the same in it. Being in love brings harmony with what is because there's no preferable alternative that could be held in mind. There is no tension between what is and what's desired, as they are in agreement.

This agreement can be created without an object of attention. It takes a perpetual surrender to the moment to see above the perspective of conditioning. Harmony with the moment precludes thought. Thoughts are the whorls and loops of the false self. If you can let go of them for long enough, they will start to fall away. Letting go of them means surrendering to what they are not, which is what is. When you surrender your perspective, you have nothing to defend or fear losing; you are both sides of every transaction, and in the absence of fear, Love is revealed.

***

The "others" in the waking world are different points of perspective nested in the same mind's dream (reality). But for form and position, both born of circumstance, they are of the identical Seer. Consider what a two-dimensional being would see if a three-dimensional being passed through its two-dimensional plane. A 3D squirrel would look like a series of two dimensional beings (horizontal lines) flitting in and out of existence as they passed through the 2D plane, sometimes appearing to exist simultaneously in multiple 2D bodies. But it's just one higher dimensional being, expressed in a lower dimension. The four legs of the squirrel, they will coexist as four horizontal lines on the 2D plane, but these legs won't see how they are connected in the higher dimension. With their senses locked into a 2D view, they would consider themselves to be separate entities. The connections are not seen in lower dimensions, but the movements of the four lines are dependent on the will of one higher dimensional consciousness. Were one of those legs to stop trying to act independently, according to its local data, a subset of the all-knowing squirrel's knowledge, it would be in alignment with the will of the squirrel. That leg would be self-realized and understand how its movements relate to the lines born of the other legs. It would be taking cues from the 3D squirrel mind that sees from the higher dimension. The line might not know why it must do what it should, but it has surrendered to the higher will. This is like the intuition that comes when the echoes of thought resolve.

***

To a Christian

In the book you follow, The New Testament, the bad guys carried books and the good guys did not. God doesn't enter through words like magic spells. Nor does God reward righteous actions done in resistance to the individuated will, for though those actions look similar to the fruit of the Spirit, the real fruit arises from the surrendering of one's will to God, such that it is dissolved in the spiritual heart. This grows the tree from which the fruit of the Spirit arises. It's not through resisting one's own will that one aligns with God, but through surrendering it. God enters through silent surrender to the unfolding of creation. God is the stillness, and surrender to what is brings you into same. Christ went silently; He surrendered to what was, and in doing so, He showed the way of the cross. The one who is lost in thought is hiding from the cross of surrender. Losing their lives in trying to save them.

Surrender is silent harmony with what is, without hiding in the wishes for more. To do this, one often needs a proper motivation beyond a self-defeating vainglory . Several things can bring one into the moment, but persistent, emotionally-painful thoughts can be fuel for a person to surrender and let go of them, hence the beatitudes. It can also motivate them to stay out of the mental editorial that usually ends up finding something painful or nostalgic. Sometimes a traumatic event can awaken a person, give them a glimpse of being apart from the identity that takes itself to be separate from creation. The opportunity cost, in terms of peace, when true peace is felt, gives you a sense of what expands it. The innocence of inner-silence born of surrender to creation's unfolding, is what brings the awakening that yields the fruit of the spirit. There is no peace in loyalty to illusion.

***

When we are unconscious, which is to be acting through an ever-looping array of exogenously-sourced thoughts, we are acting wholly out of conditioning and DNA, and DNA is a product of the conditions that brought you a body. So in the unconscious state, the being is an echo of circumstances. We are an event that has erupted from creation, and as such, we are as charted as the comets. Our collective impact has been like that of an unconscious rust on the planet, eating away at things and leaving a residue. But this is how it works, and resisting it is born of the same illusion as is participating in it, for it is resistance that is the parent of both conditions. It is a "not resisting," that dispels illusion, because resisting can only be done from within a cloud of schemes that run counter to what is. Attention split between what is and what's desired, precludes Self-knowledge as being blind in one eye precludes depth-perception. Even beyond this, there is a barrier of forgetfulness in not having had the faculties of remembrance in the time before the veil. In fact, the very use of these faculties precludes clear seeing in that their medium is also the cloud of thought.

***

The mind is like a fuzzy hand of thought that the universe uses to play peekaboo with itself.

Awakening is to "see" the hand and move your vantage point out of it to merge with what's outside the veil. This vantage point is no point at all but ubiquity, the Self knowing all to be passing movements within itself.

***

The mind is like a shark that must keep swimming, stopping only for moments of deep sleep. The unconscious being floats in a fog of thoughts that adulterates pure awareness. It buffers consciousness from itself.

***

Why is the way so narrow? It is because belief is woven of the same fabric as the veil that hides God. Belief is thought, which can take on many aspects, none of which are love. This is why Psalm 46:10 says be still and KNOW that I am God. It doesn't say be still and think that I am God.

***

The illusion of identity, you cannot stop the fruit of it while cultivating the root of it.

***

Anticipation cannot be carried over the threshold of dreaming and waking.

***

In the poem of us, the ink and paper are the form, the words, our mind, built from experience, but neither are us. Who are we? What is watching all this? Can you find It?

***

Human failings are a byproduct of the divided state, characterized by identification with form and circumstances. The illusion is that the sum of the bodily appendages are a closed loop of Self-awareness that stands in defiance of the universe. The collective reflections of its experiences, thoughts, and emotions, constitute an identity that is the self, the protagonist in every scenario. But the Self is not content, nor form, for that which can be witnessed is not the Self.

***

Pure awareness believes exactly what it sees, and so if it sees a blend of real and imagined, its reaction will be a comparable mix of emotions and physiological responses. Thought and reality are both expressions of consciousness, but seeing them overlaid as we do obscures their true nature. It's like a picture on clear film. It looks different when folded on itself, and so if you've never seen it unfolded, you don't know how it looks. The thing we rarely see in isolation is the present, and when we do, it's because a superlative event, good or bad, has pulled attention out of thoughts. Thus, people say things like "it was like watching someone else do it," upon recounting a heroic deed. Their attention was so affixed in Now that the thoughts fell away, leaving reality's Witness to see it unfold impersonally, without the illusion of a doer. When the event is good, happiness is attributed to what grabbed attention, not our essential nature in the absence of thought.

But that's all happiness is, Self's freshest expression, undiluted by the echoes of thought. Just surrender to Now and don't resist it with the thought of how to protect it or get more. The most mundane moment offers a bounty, of which that of the greatest thought, is merely a derivative, and yet, the very sipping of this derivative denies the imbibing of the full measure of its source.

***

Of form, conditioning, and consciousness, the first two are movements within the third. But these little folds in the Self provide a reflection that creates a novel texture. The Self forms the illusion of stepping out of itself, which is done through a forgetfulness that's rendered between states. Movement is engrossing for the innocent who has forgotten, but in time, the feeling of limitation gets uncomfortable. This is what drives outward seeking. Fear is believing the illusion of the "I". The I is vulnerable and corruptible, and this drives the desire for relief through expansion. However, this quest forces the "I" thought to gird itself in concepts, which become its protectorates. They exacerbate the discomfort. The desire for infinite expansion creates great tension between what is and what's wanted. Self realization reconciles the mind to the heart, the former being dissolved into the latter.

Spiritual practice is the cultivation of an inner dexterity that can manage the currents of energy and content that arise in awareness. The ultimate end of this faculty is to resolve all vibrations that are dissonant to what is, such that the stilled consciousness can merge with it. What you see occupies very little of the space that it appears to, and what it does hold is but a vibration in consciousness called a sub atomic particle. Things are movements in energy, and we perceive only some of the spectrum.

The inner voice of discontent speaks not to the absolute state of affairs, but relative to the incrementally better. Things could be nearly perfect, and yet the inner dialogue is looking for something, maybe to some other moment. It's looking away from what it has, and so it cannot see what it has is what it is.

The juice that everyone seeks comes from within, though most don't make the connection. It comes from your Self. You won't find it in materialism, adventures, politics, romance, religion, racial ideology or any other outside pursuit. In fact, most of these activities are mutually-exclusive to Self discovery because they dead-end you into the finite and fleeting, when what you are is neither.

When the house of illusion is garlanded with pleasant thoughts and sweet things, it is a fortress from which escape is not even sought. But when the friction between what is and what's held in mind is too great, a fire in the house of thought motives an escape into Now.

If you keep your attention in the immediate sphere of possibilities, intuition will hand you answers from the depths of your subconscious.

***

We each believe that we carry a sacred fire. For some, the sanctity of that flame can exist only relative to a non-sanctified flame e.g. , the outsider, the other. But for others, the sight penetrates deeper, through the superficial and into the energetic and vibrational. Below the superficial there is one Love. To miss this is to have a perspective that has been hemmed in by thought, to believe so strongly in the surface-level of things. As if electrical appliances weren't powered by the same electricity. Like one slot car has different energy than another.

***

The sweetest part of everyone you've ever loved can be revealed within your very being. But this discovery requires the inward breaking of identification as the physical and experiential bodies that particularize the expression of consciousness.

Is this the expansiveness?

The dropping of attachment to mind and body stills consciousness of the dissonant vibration of fear that these elements hold when the illusion of the individual is believed.

This dissonance comes when what's wrongly believed to be the Self, i.e., mind and body, is subject to change (illusion of death), but the mind resists change. If the mind knew that it is truly one with what it fears will destroy it, it could be still and realize this.

This decoupling stops all the vibrations that are dissonant to the unity consciousness that is Love. The expansion is that of stillness through the individuated consciousness or mind. It is the annexation of the volatile mind space on the part of the peaceful heart.

The love you've felt is born of this inner-stillness or some gradation thereof. It comes when the moment is so good that you don't resist it, though the necessity of ideal circumstance is an illusion.

Harmony with the moment is inner-stillness, even when there is outer movement. The expansion becomes even more profound when the harmony is absolute. This is to palpably realize oneness with all, which reveals itself to be love.

***

Your form owes its existence to a causal chain that is called history. To curse even one link in that chain is to be in bondage.

***

One farmer says to the hard ground "bear fruit." Another says "If you till the soil, plant the seed, give water, add fertilizer, sunlight, and time, tree will grow and fruit will come."

***

Clarity of consciousness makes apparent the love that you already are and always have been. This clarity is born of the stillness of mind that comes when discernment denies attention to all thoughts but those that dissipate with the moment they serve.

***

I feel empty and alone.

Chances are that other feelings accompany this emptiness, unwelcome ones, and connected to those feelings are unwanted thoughts. The aloneness you feel is a separation born of the blurring-distortion that those thoughts bring to your consciousness; for in clarity, we apprehend our connection to all, and in turbulence, an isolating fog. So I point you towards the silence of no-thought and the stillness of emotional peace. To that end, surrender is the practice that brings this. Engage those feelings and surrender to them, let them make you feel how they make you feel, without reaction, without resistance, and without analyzing the thought-content that they

164

power. Do this on your exhale and feel it in your solar plexus, and then surrender that feeling to the universe. Feel it dissipate as if it were leaving through your upturned head. Then commit to keeping your focus on the moment. The moment is your safe island in the shark-infested waters of thought. Keep this practice up every time there is pain. Don't forget it. Apply it like ice on a burn. You will feel better as clarity lets in the light of the universe.

***

Separatism -The separatist who claims knowledge of Self is a deluded liar, for their identity is tied to something impermanent, the body-mind. They afford themselves no opportunity to realize what they claim to already know. They believe their identification with a certain type of body grants them exclusive ownership of a soul, when this is exactly what they deny themselves in so believing. It is like one who espouses vegetarianism while eating meat.

***

In the same sense that Newtonian physics are not quite accurate and yet, are effective tools for engineering, the words that describe realization are a mere representation of what can only be analogized. However, the conveying of direct experiences can help bring one to the threshold. At this point, the expansion of mental stillness becomes the inner-parsonage from which the teacher directly instructs from within.

***

The one who takes God to be as what he mistakes himself to be, which is a thought, will surely object to this as heresy. However, to be truly present is to truly be without a thought, a worry, a desire, a grudge, or a regret. In the absence of these idols, there is nothing but God, and God is Love. God is not your mental concept of Him. That too is an idol which hides the palpability of the Spirit! This Love is rarely apprehended because we perpetually and unknowingly chase its reflection in the objects of desire, even the thoughts of which are idols.

This is what Christ was trying to tell you when He spoke of tomorrow's troubles being for tomorrow, and when His servants told you to lay your cares upon Him, and when He said that a man is unfit for service in the Kingdom if he looks back after taking to the plow.

These pointings are all about surrender to God's will and being one with its expression. Harmony with the moment brings a clarity of consciousness that reveals the sense in which you were truly created in God's image, for your true Self is Love. And when this love is felt, He eclipses every idol you could ever chase.

***

I'm lonely.

The best part of everyone is already in you. Right now is all that anyone can truthfully promise because nothing else is real. To live in the illusion that it is any other way is the source of this loneliness.

When you realize that the moment is the eternal Self, you'll stop looking for what lies beyond it.

Peace is revealed in harmony between the wish and the circumstance. Wisdom is seeing that the wish is what must yield to bring this peace.

***

Virtue does not come from following rules, only the outward appearance of it. As Christ said, a bleached tomb is outwardly beautiful but rotten within. Virtue arises naturally in the discovery of the innermost Self, which is Love. This brings a satisfaction, a contentment that changes your priorities. It betrays the reward of outward action as a temporary reflection of Love, afforded by the lack of thought-noise that comes when novelty holds attention. But the work and attachment that go into chasing these objects and experiences magnifies the disturbances that they temporarily relieve.

The actions born of thought are as a great stone that one drops into a pool. In the center of the splash is a fleeting window of clarity as the impact pushes aside the waves, but the force of the splash itself adds more turbulence to the pool. Then a bigger rock is needed to create the next gap. It is the chasing of these pacifiers that mixes up our priorities. We don't realize that the payoff is in the stillness, not the novelty that temporarily affords it. The mark of virtue is a true lack of care for prosperity and the things of the world.

***

The mental chop that hides love can be stilled without outside things. It is the emotions below the surface that move the waves. These emotions are born of inner-resistance to what is, resistance to the moment. The waves cannot be perpetually stilled from the top by willpower. It takes a surrender to the emotions that try to countervail what is. In resistance they persist, and in surrender they resolve. Do what you must outwardly do, but inwardly, see the universe as the unfoldment of perfection. It is resistance that creates the darkness, but that very darkness is what keeps you searching. Surrender is acceptance of what your thoughts cannot change.

***

The mind is the sum of your thoughts, and these are movements in consciousness that hide Love. Stillness reveals love.

***

Getting ensnared in an unwanted thought is like being a fish. The content of the thought is the lure, and once you've bitten, your resistance is the emotion behind it. Your energy is stolen through the line of emotional resistance. The only way to get unhooked is to surrender to the emotion, to swim towards it. The last thing the angler wants is for the fish to surrender and swim towards him, as the lack of tension causes the fish to fall off the hook.

***

The venue for all gratification is internal, and this gratification is at its zenith when the mind is still. Every experience and acquisition gives some measure of stillness through the alignment of thought with reality, but the stillness is not full due to requirement of thought to facilitate acquisition. Full stillness can be discovered only in the absence of pursuit.

***

Peace is to see the illusion, know it is illusion, and let it be. Hell is to see the illusion, believe it is real, and not accept it. This is to chase the candle of an ideal while rejecting the sun of the Real. But how funny is a joke that everyone already knows? It is the ignorance of the punchline that brings the laugh. It is the tension of the bound that gives sweetness to liberation. It is the illusion of diversity that grants love its reflection, for one alone is but solitude.

***

When engaging the thought is as palatable as metal in the microwave, then you will have Self knowledge. If your thoughts do not bother you, there is no motivation to examine their nature. Blessed are the poor in spirit.

***

When the mosquito comes to you to feed, he has an anesthetic that masks his bite. This is how the mind is. Realization requires the development of "mind recognition," to see the mind arising to bite you. To catch him and swat him down before the feeding starts.

***

Sometimes floating debris will gather over the surface of a cove around the water's edge. The debris can look like solid ground, but if you step on it, you'll know it's illusion. This is how the separation of the mind works. You are still the ocean beneath the illusion of thought.

***

The racist comes in all forms, for racism is born of the ego, which is not exclusive to one race. It stems from the idea that one type of body is a superior vehicle for the expression of consciousness. However, the very attachment to form is unconsciousness, for the Self is not the body. It is a very subtle trap of the ego to say that other forms cannot be realized, while the one expressing this sentiment can never themselves be realized by virtue of harboring it.

***

What passes through the senses informs the mental projection of the world in your mind. It all resides in your head as a reconstruction. However, what also resides in your head are thoughts that are not in sync with the moment. The space taken up by these vagrant thoughts cannot be used to apprehend the full measure of creation. The recognition of thoughts as malignant junk will reverse their polarity, repelling your attention from them instead of drawing it. Without the energy of your attention, the thoughts wither. This realization is a requisite to Self realization, else you will be ever seduced by the siren of thought. You will never still the waters of consciousness that allow for Self recognition and the peace that it reveals.

***

The Satanist, the Christian, the atheist, and agnostic all revere something represented by a thought. The first two worship the concepts of deities, and the latter two, thought itself, represented as reason. God is palpably realized in the absence of concepts. The devil that blocks man from God is man's very concept of God, for concepts are thoughts, a blanket that hides God. There can be no silence in thought, no stillness, and therefore, only dissonance to God's will, which is found in the moment. Silence of mind is surrender to God's will.

***

The cloak of personality is as unique as a fingerprint but all personalities are weaved of impressions and have the property of obscuring the peace of pure awareness. The more malignant personalities are those to which diagnoses can be attached. Others are more "normal," but suffer similar frailties, though to lesser degrees. However, all personalities are opaque to the luminous awareness which they envelope. The thicker the illusion of personality, the more it takes for the person to realize their own joy. Such persons are more driven to seek the illusion of an outer source of light and quickly become jaded. Thinner personalities also seek outside but can feel more of the inner glow, and are thus more stable in their attachments/relationships. To realize the true source of peace, the personality must fall away as a lampshade that hides the bulb.

***

The perceived correctness of knowledge doesn't dispel its opacity relative to the Self. The more correct ones knowledge is believed to be, the less likely its holder is to realize the Self. The Self is not knowledge, but It is the holder who is hidden by knowledge by way of unconscious identification as it; therefore, knowledge that reveals its false nature can be discarded. In this way, the fool who realizes they are a fool can stop trusting their knowledge, discard it by way of surrender and inadvertently discover who

171

they truly are. It's the one whose knowledge has never betrayed them who stays blinded by it. He is as the camel trying to pass through the eye of the needle.

***

The dogmatist fails to grasp that different words mean the same thing to different people. I can give two sets of directions that lead to the same place by describing different landmarks to different people, based on which have meaning to them. All that matters is that those words lead to the destination. And truly, this destination is silence, a purity of spirit that is devoid of words as we understand them.

***

The animal brain has no discernment, but it directly precipitates the body's survival reactions. The mind's imagined scenarios trigger real reactions in the animal brain. Thoughts tell the lower brain when various stress hormones should be released into the bloodstream. The animal brain's role as the body's pharmacist, combined with its lack of discernment, poses a huge invisible problem for the human being. This is because the upper brain is out of control, and everything it projects to the animal brain is believed, and thus, the animal brain poisons us.

A being who cannot control their thoughts and stay quiet inside is like a machine whose operating system has been hijacked by an outside controller. The control mechanism is the imaginary content that takes up residence in the mind, e.g., every bit of carefully crafted and edited brainwashing that's projected through various media outlets. Everything you are taught, and all of the commercials designed to sharpen your appetites. It's the sexualized content that makes the reproductive function go haywire and the violent images that turn on fight or flight. It's the programmed tribal conflicts taught in the news and academia that stereotype strangers as malcontents or oppressors.

What if there was no script? What if we simply turned it all off and had to take each person we met as an individual and could hold them accountable for nothing but our actual, real-time interaction and not what the agitators and media masters told us about their kind of person? What if we dealt only with the actual person when they were before us and never with the concept of them or their "kind?"

We would see each person with new eyes and not ones jaded by instigators. None but a quiet mind can do this. See the hands on your mind, see the instigator who wants you to buy his wares to escape the fears he placed in you. See the political animals who cultivate tribalism as a means of securing their personal power. You can break them all by separating yourself from their message, by unplugging them from your brain, living in no place but the here and now. The looping thoughts must be stopped by surrendering to the moment.

***

Truly making love to someone is helping them see the love they already are. Beneath the noisy ripples of uncontrolled thought lies an ocean of love that is us, but not one in a million beings palpably apprehends this.

When you are aware that you are pure awareness, the ripples of thought have stilled, and this perspective is the only possible common denominator, for all other thoughts are like snowflakes that will never totally match. Only utter stillness of consciousness can be faithfully reproduced. Then you are in unity with every stilled mind. You are one with every sage.

***

Emotional pain is like the potential energy that can be used for the purpose of breaking the ego as a vase that may fall from a great height. The weight of the ego also contributes to its destruction. Surrender from great pain is as a fall of a heavy and brittle object from a great height. If there is no pain, it is as if the vase sits on the ground with no potential energy. This is why it is hard for a rich man to enter heaven. And why "blessed are the poor in spirit."

***

When the roads of time have not been trodden, love and awareness remain unsodden.

***

The lightening of emotional pain is conducted into the feet of attention when they stand in the water of thought.

***

The dogmatist is like one who insists that clothing must be of a certain name brand, while he walks around naked. If through the same practice of surrender, two saints discover the same unity that destroys all concepts, the names given by each will be known as mere nominalizations. It is the ones who come after, reading the stories but never having had the realization, who want to fight over names.

***

The more secure the circumstances of a life, the greater the opportunity to be lost in illusion. Security enhances the fallacy that impermanent things can be made permanent. It affords the luxury of ignorance. Why see the truth of the unreal, and thus, the real, if you don't have to? The unreal is anything that can change or dissolve, which is all but the single incorruptible awareness, but security hides this fact by providing some assurance of a delayed departure. It pushes the truth of impermanence far enough out on the horizon that it can be ignored for a time. The idea of security is both a product of attachment and a contributor to it. The work that goes into creating security is deemed to be a worthy cause by the one who's attached to the thing being secured. But this work also reinforces the sense of separation, as it involves much thought, much disturbing of consciousness, which obscures the knowledge of Self within the frothy whitecaps of mental churn. Who can know themselves when they turn away from the real and wallow in the false?

***

Like a balloon squeezed on one end or the other, karma will play out in either the dreaming or the waking.

***

The forms are movements within the field of consciousness. The intelligence that gives rise to them can be likened to gravity. Just as there is one gravitational principle acting upon myriad forms according to their respective conditions, there is likewise one intelligence acting through them. The insentient forms are members of the whole, and the sentient are granted the illusion of a perspective born of circumstance.

The seemingly inert forms are like still objects that in gravitational terms, contain potential energy, but in conscious terms, they contain potential individuation, but until the causal chain spins them off into the mirrored room of self-awareness, they abide as limbs of the whole intelligence.

This would describe the chain of events by which soil becomes plants and are then converted to flesh through consumption. Consider an avalanche of little rocks, each moves as if of its own accord, but the gravity that moves them is one. Likewise, consider all individual beings, the expressions are myriad and react in accordance with precise conditions. However, when bereft of all conditioning and circumstance, they are one, like the uniform electricity that flows from the power outlet but causes each machine to act differently, depending on how the power is channeled by the circuits and programming of the machine.

The free being has merged into the homogeneous intelligence before the unraveling of the form it inhabits. This is the reversion into the stillness and silence of love. The opposite is the vortex of separation.

***

The knowledge that leads to freedom is of the kind that dispels the attachment to knowledge, including itself. It leads to silence and not the noise of thought. There is no heresy in true inner-silence, nor in the teaching that brings it. It is thought that disturbs consciousness and brings dissonance with creation. Inner silence is the only acquiescence to God's will. All else is the fruit of the knowledge of good and evil. All else is in resistance to creation. All else thinks it knows better. The knowledge that leads to truth points to inner silence, all else will eventually want to take something from you because it is lacking and seeking in the wrong direction, outward and not inward.

***

The body is consciousness that holds a sandbox of consciousness that we call mind. The sand is the body of thoughts in which the awareness plays. Awareness plays in this sandbox of mental objects and merges with it, believes it is part of the sand, but sometimes the glass of troubled thoughts get in the sandbox and dispels the illusion. Sometimes there is so much glass that awareness must get out of the sandbox.

***

Why are people less courteous behind the wheel than while walking the halls? It is because the barrier of the car itself creates an additional layer of separation. The same principal applies in identification with the superficial sheaths of the body. The elements of a being are: the gross body, the thought body, the intelligence that measures them, the energy body, and the heart. It's the identification with the physical and thought bodies that brings separation and thus, ill treatment of perceived others. The reason for this is that these two aspects are both unique and temporary. In their uniqueness they do not harmonize completely with others, and in their temporal nature, identification with them brings fear of disintegration. Fear and love are mutually exclusive, and in the stillness of consciousness, love is the witnesses all five sheaths of the body. The knowledge that you are none of these sheaths, but rather, their witness, is like stepping out of the car. The witness loves everything, including the car, and wishes it no ill, but it has less fear for itself when it has stepped outside of identification with it. When you are in the car, the prospect of its destruction is more troubling than when you're outside of it. All of these bodily sheaths will grow when attention is given to them, but attention must be removed from the fearful aspects and given to the heart in order for it to grow in the likeness of its witness. The light of attention must not pass through the prism of thought if the heart is to grow in the likeness of its loving witness.

Made in the USA
San Bernardino, CA
23 November 2018